To My Baby Sister on Her Big 50

Diane

ON WOMEN TURNING 50

Celebrating Mid-Life Discoveries

CATHLEEN ROUNTREE

HarperSanFrancisco

A Division of HarperCollinsPublishers

To Christian

To all the women who lit the path before me

And to all those who will follow

This book is dedicated.

HarperSanFrancisco and the author, in association with the Rainforest Action Network, will facilitate the planting of two trees for every one tree used in the manufacture of this book.

ON WOMEN TURNING FIFTY: *Celebrating Mid-Life Discoveries.* Copyright © 1993 by Cathleen Rountree. All rights reserved. Printed in the United States of America. No part of this book may be used or reproduced in any manner whatsoever without written permission except in the case of brief quotations embodied in critical articles and reviews. For information address HarperCollins Publishers, 10 East 53rd Street, New York, NY 10022.

HarperCollins books may be purchased for educational, business, or sales promotional use. For information, please call or write: Special Markets Department, HarperCollins Publishers, Inc., 10 East 53rd Street, New York, NY 10022. Telephone: (212) 207-7528; Fax: (212) 207-7222.

FIRST HARPERCOLLINS PAPERBACK EDITION

Library of Congress Cataloging-in-Publication Data

Rountree, Cathleen.
On women turning fifty : celebrating mid-life discoveries / Cathleen Rountree.
   p. cm.
ISBN 0-06-250668-4
1. Middle aged women–United States. I. Title
HQ1059.5U5R684 1993   92–54617
305.24'4–dc20   CIP

93 94 95 96 97 ❖ RRD–H 10 9 8 7 6 5 4 3 2 1

This edition is printed on acid-free paper that meets the American National Standards Institute Z39.48 Standard.

Contents

There are certain individuals who, in the process of resolving their own inner conflicts, become paradigms for broader groups.

ERIK ERIKSON

Acknowledgments

So many thanks to give!

How can I properly thank Ellen Levine, my literary agent, for your loyalty and validation, or Amy Hertz, my editor at Harper San Francisco, for your vision and encouragement? Warriors both, you have brought miracles into my life, and have been instrumental in teaching me that "The harder I work, the luckier I am." Thank you.

My friendship with Linda Leonard is both deepening and refining to my emotional, spiritual, and intellectual life; and knowing Allie Light and Irving Saraf has contributed to my well-being during the work on this project. Thank you.

Thanks, also, to photographers and friends: Gypsy Ray for your patient directives, and Ruth Morgan for your unfailing "eye."

Thanks, Susan Drake, for your invaluable transcribing. And my and Sienna's warm gratitude to Janmarie Silvera, the director of "Camp Aromas."

I wish to thank wholeheartedly the women in this book who shared your time and insights with me as well as with every woman and man who will read this book. It is a privilege to know you.

Every reader of this book has her own story. It is my hope that you will find parts of yourself in each chapter, that you will find the truth within yourself, for that truth will be your source of strength and beauty.

As always, gratitude to my very dear circle of friends who have supported me, listened to me, teased me, tolerated me, sustained me, urged me on, and celebrated with me. I love you all.

And, finally, I especially thank my son, Christian, and our friend, Jana, for your love, enthusiasm, and sound practical counsel in times both good and challenging.

Blessings on you all.

Introduction

Once women pass fifty, if they can avoid the temptations of the eternal youth purveyors, the sellers of unnatural thinness and cosmetic surgery, they may be able to tap into the feisty girls they once were. And if, at adolescence, the importance of their own convictions had been reinforced, they might, at fifty, be ready to take on risk, display a new-found vitality, and bid goodbye to conventional limitations.

CAROLYN HEILBRUN, The New York Times Book Review

I've known younger women who were only forty and older than I was at fifty. Fifty? Who's talking about fifty? That's youth. That's at the very crest of success. No, not the crest, for that would indicate the subsiding, the demise. Fifty is simply young. It has health. Beauty. A rich background of talents and the means to express them. Fifty is strong. Fifty is the end of the burdens of retarded childhood, one's own and one's children's. It is freedom from menstruation. It is full of power. It is being totally alive and having plenty of time to be alive.

LOUISE MATTLAGE, Women and Aging

THEA SKOLVER WAS FIFTY-THREE YEARS OLD when, in the spring of 1992, she jumped from her ninth-floor apartment on the East side of midtown Manhattan and landed in a bed of red tulips. "I'm out of the loop in every way," read her suicide note. "Both professionally and personally. I really don't belong anywhere!"

"I don't belong anywhere!" The words are chilling. And for those women who find themselves in a similar situation to Thea's they sound even more ominous. Thea feared that because of her age, she would fail to find a permanent male partner. She worried that she could not support herself and would become a homeless pauper. She felt isolated and without friends who really cared about her. And she had become depressed during her menopause, which added fuel to her fears. Thea was right: with no meaningful work or creative outlet, without a significant relationship or nurturing women friends, without a spiritual connection to nature or an inner life, she didn't belong—because she didn't belong to herself.

Like Thea, I too have my fears of growing old alone. The pathetic images of a bag lady or of a lonely old woman abandoned in a rest home sometimes cross my mind when I think about my future. But I have learned to calm many of my fears about aging by simplifying my life, by learning to enjoy my solitude, by redefining my definition of success, by valuing my friendships with women, by cultivating my inner life through a spiritual connection to nature and a creative expression, and by trying my best to be alive in the present moment. It's not always easy, but it makes life much richer and thwarts depression, to which I am inclined.

Our attitudes and fears are formed by our society. Thea Skolver's friend Audrey Flack said of her, "She bought society's line. She wanted success, grandeur, glamour. But you can have a good life with simpler things. The myth she followed has to be exposed, broken."

In writing *On Women Turning Fifty: Celebrating Mid-life Discoveries*, I set out to expose and help break the myths about middle-aged women. For the past twenty-five to thirty years, through the politicizing and restructuring of their individual lives, American women have been largely responsible for shifting many cultural paradigms. They have demanded equal rights in the work force, shared responsibilities in the home, and taken control over their bodies' reproduction. In the process we have begun to redefine the parameters of age and reexamine its cultural mythology.

We are living during a period in modern history when the Feminine is breaking through in Western culture with phenomenal force in the areas of politics, education, art, business, and the sciences. *On Women Turning Fifty* presents the stories of dedicated women between the ages of fifty and sixty who share concerns for and visions of a new world. As conversations bring to light unconscious attitudes, the women interviewed inevitably discover what is valid and valuable about their life experiences.

American society, with its emphasis on youth and sexuality as a woman's primary assets, sees the individual woman as becoming less and less valuable as she grows older. Indeed, she becomes almost invisible. In her book *The Beauty Myth* (New York: William Morrow, 1991), Naomi Wolf observes that women's magazines "ignore older women or pretend they don't exist: magazines try to avoid photographs of older women, and when they feature celebrities who are over forty, 'retouching artists' conspire to 'help' beautiful women look more beautiful; i.e., less their age." Thus we see that looks are a currency, and according to this monetary system, the older a woman gets, the more cash-poor she becomes.

Magazine readers and moviegoers have no idea what a real woman's forty- or fifty-year-old face looks like because photographers use lighting techniques, makeup, and other technical tricks to make sure older women appear ten to fifteen years younger in print and in films. Worse, we then look in the mirror and think we look too old for our age, because we're comparing ourselves to the retouched face that smiles at us from a magazine or a wide screen.

Wolf, in her polemic treatise, sums it up: "To airbrush age off a woman's face is to erase women's identity, power, and history. . . . We as women are trained to see ourselves as cheap imitations of fashion photographs, rather than seeing fashion photographs as cheap imitations of women." In my conversation with Sumahsil, a ceremonialist who helps women celebrate menopause through ritual, she told me, "We spend so much time in denial and not accepting our bodies or fighting weight. We have to make a new vision of what a beautiful woman is—each of us—and appreciate ourselves."

The irony is that during her middle years, when a woman is no longer seen as a sexual *object,* she begins to experience herself as a truly sexual *being.* In our late forties and early fifties, with the onset of menopause, we enter a season in which we no longer need concern ourselves with unwanted pregnancy and birth control. We become more concerned with female production rather than *re*production. Many women have informed me that it wasn't until their fifties that they began to enjoy sex in a more liberating and carefree manner, partly because of this factor. We are no longer dominated by the hormones that drive our sexual passions. As Gloria Steinem says in this book, "Aging has brought me freedom from romance; freedom from the ways in which your hormones distort your judgment and make you do things that aren't right for you. Going through menopause makes the difference."

On Women Turning Fifty gives women entering the middle years a variety of role models to contemplate and hold as positive internal images, to replace the deprecating pictures currently projected by society. It is my hope that the conversations in this book will provide you with a feeling of pride and strength in your maturity, and that they will offer alternative ways of perceiving both your body image and your internal image and of viewing your role as a professional woman, wife, mother, or friend.

Women in their fifties have come to care more about how *they feel* than about what *others think.* This shift in how one meets the world can be enormously liberating for women who may have spent decades performing physically depleting and spiritually uninspiring work, running a household, and being responsible for growing children or an expectant mate.

If a woman is fortunate, the fifties can be a breakthrough time in which she learns to reconcile being alone and faces her own mortality. "We have to realize we can only die by ourselves," said documentary filmmaker Allie Light. The issues of women in their fifties are vast, complex, and increasingly urgent, as Thea Skolver's life and death made clear. As one woman I interviewed put it: "I'm on the edge of looking for something and afraid I won't find it." Pressed to explain just exactly *what* she is looking for, she mentioned meaningful work, a satisfying relationship, lasting friendships, and inner contentment.

To several generations of women who bought stock in the myth "Someday my prince will come," the eventual awakening of "the princess" can be a purgatorial passage into the rest of a life devoted exquisitely to herself and to a life of the inner being. "I realized I had to seriously accept the possibility that I might spend the rest of my life without a man," said one woman in her midfifties who had been divorced and lived alone for more than twenty years. If that were to be the case, she realized, she'd better forge ahead and begin to take seriously her avocation of creative writing. In the past she'd given it only minimal attention, devoting most leisure time to her physical maintenance in the hope of attracting a man.

Several of the women with whom I spoke have remained married to their first or second husbands and have crafted enduring and mutually supportive relationships. Some, like Isabel Allende, found love in their late forties or fifties. Allende says, "My husband and I got together very late in our lives, and we discovered a passionate love affair. There *is* passion for older women in midlife. Absolutely!" Numerous women have found loving and committed relationships with other women. As they turn fifty, women who have been recently divorced or have never married may be coming to terms with the possibility that they will spend the rest of their lives alone. I interviewed several single women in their fifties who have actually come to prefer their solitary lives. Many women have lived alone for so many years that they don't know if they *could* live with a spouse or a partner again—or if they'd want to. "I do exactly as I please, whenever I please, with whomever I please. Why would I want to forfeit that independence?" said a fifty-three-year-old publicist who lives in Seattle, Washington.

One of the benefits of the past twenty-five years of the Women's Liberation Movement has been women's emergence from a despairing sense of loneliness and isolation. When women began opening up to each other, they realized they were no longer alone, and the gift of sharing female friends and companionship with each other has become a necessity of varying degrees to all the women in this book. Jungian analyst Dr. Jean Shinoda Bolen told me, "What often hasn't been acknowledged by women is the depth and importance of their friendships with one another. When you're going through a difficult time in your life, who do you confide in? Do you speak to your husband or your best friend?"

The need to deepen the spiritual dimension of our lives may become apparent to us in our forties, when we begin to lose parents, partners, and friends; but in our fifties we are faced with the unavoidable realization of our *own* transience, when the severity of our abuse (consciously or through ignorance) to our bodies and souls can no longer be denied. It is also especially difficult to ignore this awareness in the decade of our fifties, during which the loss of a parent occurs more frequently than in any other age group.

At fifty-one, noted photographer Mary Ellen Mark told me, "I feel full of energy and physically as strong as I've ever been. I feel very fit." However, illness and a noticeable waning of physical strength may begin to hit women during their sixth decade in startling or frightening ways. According to the National Cancer Institute, one in eight American women will get breast cancer during her life. And the risk increases with age: about 80 percent of breast cancers develop in women over fifty. That still leaves lung and uterine cancer and heart disease, which are major causes of death among women in their fifties.

In her autobiography, *And a Voice to Sing With* (New York: Summit Books, 1987), Joan Baez wrote, "You don't get to choose how you're going to die. Or when. You can only decide how you're going to live. Now." Facing one's own mortality can bring a kind of freedom. When we finally confront our fear of dying and eventually accept our solitude, women can discover a new self-confidence. Then all the conventional limitations, of which Carolyn Heilbrun speaks, that formerly constricted our behavior fall away. This is when our freedom to be who we truly are emerges. The fifties can be the beginning of the most creative period in our lives. Through this newly gained confidence and creativity comes true iconoclasm. The women in this book fully celebrate their iconoclasm as breakers of negative cultural images and myths. They begin new careers, say goodbye to passionless marriages, open themselves (perhaps for the first time) to a spiritual life, and begin new activities—whatever it is *they* want to do, be it painting or belly dancing or sky-diving.

The necessity for developing an inner life and a creative expression become increasingly important in a woman's middle years, and can provide a sanctuary through the "joyful participation in the sorrows of the world," as Joseph Campbell witnessed in *A Fire in the Mind* (New York: Doubleday, 1992). The act of creating can clear confusion by allowing us to focus our energies, and offers a way to express our personal voice. When a woman touches that center of genuine emotion and imagination within her, life takes on another dimension, in which the inner life begins to dictate the outer existence.

Because women tend to put themselves in categories (perhaps because we have been so categorized by our cultures), we perceive ourselves and our issues as different from decade to decade. In many ways, however, the years bridging a woman's forties and fifties are interlaced like an intricate arabesque pattern, sharing common psychological, emotional and spiritual relevance. Simultaneously young and old, according to the French novelist Victor Hugo,

> The forties are the old age of youth,
> While the fifties are the youth of old age.

Developing a strong identity amid so many confusing cultural images of femininity is an ongoing struggle for most young women, and is often in conflict with the standard of beauty and femininity that we see reflected all around us. But by the time women reach their fifties, they've either come to terms with the cultural derision of their developing "crow's feet," "turkey necks," and "cottage-cheese thighs," or opted for the surgeon's scalpel. Those who choose to follow the purveyors of eternal youth, however, pay a price: their fundamental fear and anxiety, which initially prompted their resort to plastic surgery, continues to consume them from the inside out, as they reject the inevitable process of aging.

When I lived in Los Angeles for four years during the 1980s, I found an alarming number of women (many of them only in their twenties and thirties) who had succumbed to plastic surgery. It saddened me to see women (none of whom showed many signs of inner contentment) who hated their bodies to such an extreme that they would resort to self-mutilation. In order to ensure my own refusal to partake of this pervasive and perverse "service," whenever I noticed that my décolletage was sagging, that my eyelids were drooping, or that my derriere was dimpling beyond acceptable L.A. standards, I would sit in a corner of my mind droning a mantra that I'd conjured as self-defense: "Happiness is the best face-lift. Happiness is the best face-lift. Happiness is the best face-lift."

This is no joke. My overall view of the "good life" in Southern California became decidedly unglamorous and even pathetic. Los Angeles (and increasingly, other metropolitan cities) is filled with middle- and upper-middle-class Americans straining to stay young through aerobics, obsessive dieting (a $33-billion-a-year industry), compulsive use of cosmetics (a $20-billion-a-year industry), and plastic surgery (a $300-million-a-year industry). What these women have failed to fathom is that youth has everything to do with the *spirit* and the *mind,* and much less to do with age. Wendy Wasserstein, the Pulitzer Prize-winning playwright of *The Heidi Chronicles* and *The Sisters Rosensweig,* has said, "Nobody in Hollywood says, 'Oh, boy—let's do a play about a fifty-four-year-old woman who falls in love, who still has possibilities' " (*New York Times,* Oct. 18, 1992).

Concerns about money and retirement seem to increase exponentially with age—and with good reason. Women over sixty-five are the fastest-growing segment of the United States population, and one in five lives in poverty. "If you are a woman," writes one economist, "you have a 60 percent shot at being poor in old age." One woman I interviewed asked, "Will I end up as a bag lady?"

Economic independence is basic to a feeling of personal dignity. Most women in their fifties see their financial future looming rather menacingly, because we live in a society where people who don't earn money don't count. By the time a woman turns fifty, she has fifteen years (in the establishment's time-frame) until the official age of retirement. If she hasn't done so already, she can still pursue an alternative "workstyle" during these years, in order to fill her days, and thus her life, with purpose, as well as to augment her established income.

This is also a time when women may begin seriously thinking about whether they want to live alone or consciously to become part of an extended family or a supportive community in order to reduce their living expenses (as well as their potential loneliness). In her fifties Deanne Burke, a single mother and grammar-school teacher living in Berkeley, California, recently bought a duplex with another single mother. She is convinced that this "tenant-in-common" arrangement "*can* work for people."

Grasping the truth in poet and novelist Annie Dillard's words— "How we spend our days is how we spend our lives"—women prefer to make a *living* rather than to follow the norm of our capitalist/consumer oriented society, to "make a *killing*." They are more likely to choose work because of its daily emotional satisfaction rather than its financial reward. At the age of fifty, and after raising her three sons as a single mother, Claire Braz-Valentine took the opportunity offered by her employer for early retirement in order to write and teach in a prison. As she describes it, "I figured if I stayed at the job and got used to having all that money just for myself that I would never live my dream of being a full-time writer. I held onto the dream."

Several women with whom I spoke have been creative in developing meaningful ways to support themselves. They began to think solemnly about what it is that engages them and how they like to spend their time. One woman I know spent years attending medical school to become a veterinarian, but then found it difficult to deal with the business-oriented, overpriced clinics where she first worked. Within a few years, she made the commitment to change her working situation and is now self-employed as a "traveling vet," visiting her canine clients at their homes. She makes her own schedule and chooses her clients. People are so grateful for her sincere concern for their animals' health care, her reasonable prices, and her peripatetic practice that she reluctantly has to turn clients away.

Thirty years ago Susan Drake graduated from college with a degree in creative writing, and during those years she continued to write poetry and short stories while working as a secretary to support herself and her children. Finally, in her early fifties, she realized that the price she was paying for the ostensible security of a weekly paycheck was too high. She decided to operate her own transcribing business from her home, working only with writers whose work stimulates her. Now she is self-supporting, and she has more incentive and more time for her private writing, which has resulted in several published articles.

Both of these women admit that changing their "workstyle" was not easy, and at first demanded even more time than their conventional jobs. But they agree that the subsequent rewards far outweigh the intensity of the initial hard work and terror that they might not survive. The element of choice in their lives is essential to these women. Jean Shinoda Bolen concurs, "The choices we make determine who we become, offering us the possibility of leading an authentic life."

We all have certain activities that we enjoy. We each have several talents, one or more of which can be segued into a service to offer others. This is the meaning of "right livelihood." On the wall above my desk, I keep a list on which I jot down any spontaneous thoughts about making a living that come to me. The growing list is a reminder that my options are diverse. In Ibsen's *Ghosts* a character proclaims, "The joy of life and the love of one's work are practically the same thing." This is success.

Perhaps, for those of us who are now bringing the twentieth century to a close, the construct of success needs to be deconstructed, resimplified. I recently came across this journal entry I'd written several years ago: "I've never felt successful. I don't own an impressive car, my own home, expensive art, extravagant clothes. But I'm a working artist and writer who meets life creatively. I'm healthy. I live in a beautiful environment, close to nature. My son is most important to me. I have loving and supportive friends, many of whom think I live like a rich person, because I do and have just about everything I want on practically nothing. (Still, I worry about money.) I travel frequently. I have a spiritual practice that nourishes me. I love my dog. Life is infinitely interesting. Maybe *I'm* okay, but my *definition* of success is wrong for me." Since then I've begun to think of myself as "independently wealthy" because I realize that I carry within myself most of what I need to make me happy.

In the workshops I've offered for several years, I have found that women are comforted to hear the stories of other women and grateful to see how those women have changed their lives. Living examples remain the best source of inspiration. My involvement with these women demonstrates to me again how hungry women are for personal stories that inspire and invite introspection, and confirms my belief that we better understand and give shape to ourselves by reading about and studying other women's lives. I have also come to realize that women *do* perceive themselves and their issues differently in the various decades.

At some point in every woman's life, the identity she has worked so hard to project comes into question. In the 1950s a woman's path was often demarcated by her husband, children, and family ties. Popular magazines such as *Good Housekeeping* and *Ladies' Home Journal* supported the code of duplicity that dominated the era, a code that required hiding resentment at her loss of identity to a husband and family. Authenticity was seen as revealing oneself in poor taste. This was the prevalent social attitude in which women who are now in their fifties and sixties were reared, and out of which the concept of consciousness-raising and the first wave of the Women's Liberation Movement emerged. Theirs was a pivotal generation. Groomed for marriage and motherhood, they entered the business world, the professions of medicine and law, often raising children alone, while paving the way for younger women.

Ageism is a final frontier, the last metaphorical girdle from which women must free themselves. But aging is a process to be met in stages. Each decade in one's life can provide a renewed opportunity (the next step in that march to the inevitable) to comprehend the meaning of one's own personal process of aging—those future possibilities that we have yet to dream and ignite, and those fantasies we must recognize as forever unattainable and ultimately release. Each decade can also provide an occasion to encourage, assist, and participate with other women in a mutual effort to increase our self-worth, enabling each of us to offer the gift of our unique contribution to the global community. In a study of women over fifty who had never been married, the most important purpose or value they listed was social responsibility. In their fifties women are ready to share their gifts.

"I don't even know what fifty is supposed to look like!" shrugged Coeleen Kiebert, an artist, whose flawless complexion, natural blond hair, elegance, and sense of style are stunning; an ageist would place her at easily ten years below her fifty-nine. So what *does* fifty look like? There are as many answers to this question as there are women who ask it. *On Women Turning Fifty* focuses on the issues in middle-aged women's lives, affirms the promise of a fulfilling mid-life when a woman truly nurtures the vast creative and spiritual resources within herself, and reveals the visions of eighteen effective women who have made distinctive, expressive, and meaningful lives for themselves. It is their spirit of aliveness that these stories are about. While we are fortunate to have such role models, the responsibility remains within each of us to discover the spirit of aliveness within ourselves. *On Women Turning Fifty* provides an inspiring companion for those who undertake the journey of mid-life transformation. Perhaps if a friend had given a book like this to Thea Skolver, she wouldn't have felt so alone. Just as the women in this book have done, she might have developed those areas in her life which could have nurtured her and helped save her life. She may have learned to welcome solitude, instead of dreading it. As Academy Award-winning actress Ellen Burstyn told me, "Solitude has become very important to me. That seems to come with the fifties."

In *Journal of a Solitude,* May Sarton wrote, "The garden is growth and change and that means loss as well as constant new treasures to make up for a few disasters."

Tending a garden is a natural metaphor for cultivating an inner life. The art of cultivating—a garden, a child, an art form, a lover or one's soul—can nurture the landscape of our lives, transforming a barren survival into a fruitful existence.

Writing this book has been a way of cultivating my future, which includes my inevitable aging—tilling the soil, planting the seeds, feeding and watering early naked shoots in the private Giverny of my mind and heart. This interior garden has been fostered by the gift of elder wisdom from each woman presented in this book who, by developing her intrinsic inner authority, speaks the truth of her own life, thus inspiring and empowering others to do the same. It is my vision that the seeds which I have planted in this metaphorical garden will, by the time I turn fifty, blossom into a prism of new treasures.

I offer you a garden of treasures.

CATHLEEN ROUNTREE

Aptos, California
October 1992

ELLEN BURSTYN

Solitude. Blessed solitude has become very important to me. I find that when I have a day alone, I just revel in it, indulge in it, bathe in it. It's the most incredible luxury. That seems to come with the fifties.

profile

I FIRST DISCOVERED ELLEN BURSTYN IN 1972 in *The King of Marvin Gardens,* a film directed by Bob Rafelson. She played the role of Sally, a once beautiful woman now past her prime and tragically anxious to prevent the defection of her lover. In one scene Sally burns her store of cosmetics on the beach at Atlantic City. Even though I was only twenty-four at the time, that scene affected me deeply; it spoke piercingly of how one lonely and frightened woman found the courage to deal with what Carolyn Heilbrun would later call "the tyranny of the male gaze."

Born Edna Rae Gilooly in Detroit, Michigan, Ellen Burstyn's illustrious career has encompassed stage, film, and television. She became something of a feminist icon in 1974 after her Academy Award-winning portrayal of an ex-housewife turned waitress/singer trying to support herself and her twelve-year-old son, in the film *Alice Doesn't Live Here Anymore.* By then, as a single mother myself, the portrait of Alice and her struggles—emotional, financial and spiritual—seemed familiar and poignant.

Burstyn played many other leading roles (and earned four more Academy Award nominations) in such memorable movies as *The Last Picture Show, The Exorcist, Alex in Wonderland, Harry and Tonto, Same Time Next Year,* and *Twice in a Lifetime.* Her stage roles included *Same Time Next Year* (for which she won a Tony Award), *84 Charing Cross Road, Driving Miss Daisy,* and *Shirley Valentine.* But the film that has been most unforgettable to me, and which I most readily associate with Ellen Burstyn, is her role as Edna McCauley in the 1980 film *Resurrection,* based on a concept originally conceived by Ellen and written for her by Lewis Carlino. The title refers to Edna's recovery from a near-fatal car crash and her return to life with the Christ-like gift of healing through the power of love. But the title is also a metaphor for the numerous metamorphoses that Edna (and many women in their middle years) experiences: she heals her unhappy childhood, she discovers her true identity and inner authority, she becomes free of social restrictions and outside ex-pectations, she finds a life of meaning through service to her community, and she no longer lets her life revolve around a man. Deftly combining mysticism and fem-inism, it is the film that made me most interested in meeting Ellen Burstyn.

At four o'clock on a crisp and clear autumn afternoon, after six months of trying to arrange a mutually convenient meeting time and place, I was finally going to meet

Ellen Burstyn. Our designated meeting place was the Actors Studio on West 44th Street in New York City, home to some of the most famous names in American acting. The Actors Studio had been started by Lee Strasberg, the famous drama coach associated with such luminaries as Marilyn Monroe, Marlon Brando, Robert DeNiro, and Ellen Burstyn. Ellen served as the Artistic Director for six years, and continues to be active there as a member of the Executive Board of Directors.

That day she was dressed in layers of natural fabrics in a variety of textures and patterns in black and white. Her shoes were red, white, and black, and whimsical. I remember thinking that Dorothy would be pleased to wear them on her way to Oz. Red hair, fine and short, framed green eyes, wide cheekbones, and a dazzling smile. We went for a bite at the corner restaurant, Southwest, where we settled in at a window table for nearly three hours.

Within half an hour, I was having so much fun that I forgot I was with a "movie star." Ellen assured me that actors are incorrigible people watchers, and she sat staring out at the passersby as I photographed her. Quick both to find amusement and to be amusing, Ellen pointed out an elderly man standing at the street corner waiting for the light to change. All of his life was right there in his body, twitching and turning, full of expression. "That's basically what actors do," she explained, "study people—their outer manifestations and their psychology. That's why it's so interesting, that's really the art form: people-playing."

It was tough not to notice those who thought they recognized Ellen Burstyn. They would walk past our table three or four times, trying not to be noticed, to be cool, but their wandering eyes were a dead giveaway. At last, nodding their heads in positive identification, their lips would form the words, "Yep, that's Ellen Burstyn." Ellen told me how she used to tire of being noticed, until fewer people recognized her and then she missed them.

Like many of the characters she plays, Ellen Burstyn has undergone and continues to experience transformation and liberation. She shares with many of her film personae certain traits—notably, humor and a determination to be herself. When I asked her about her fantasy of aging, she responded, "I really want to embody the crone. Remember the last scene of *Resurrection?* That's what I want to be. I want to have wild white hair and bones clinking as I walk and moccasins on my feet and jewels and young poets at my feet."

*I*T'S IMPORTANT FOR WOMEN TO LEARN from our experiences; not necessarily our happy experiences, but from the painful ones. When I teach actors, I tell them, "Your life experiences are raw material. When you transform your experiences into meaning or art, you've taken the process and used it in a creation. If you are able to do that, you say, 'Thank God I had an unhappy childhood!'" Otherwise, they're just experiences. To treat your unhappy childhood as a pathology and continue to try to cure it—which we've all been trying to do for the last twenty-five years or more—keeps us at the same level: "Oh, I wish my Daddy or Mommy loved me, but they didn't. How can I make up for that loss?" But if you can find a way to penetrate the surface of those experiences and start to discern the pattern, find the meaning in the pattern—the sort of crazy quilt of your life—then you transform your life into a work of art and understand that the most horrible experiences are the biggest learning tools.

In my own life, some of those motivating experiences have been an unhappy childhood, three unhappy marriages, failures. I've learned from all my failures—not all, but most of my learning has come from my failures. I don't know if you learn much from success or happiness. They are very nice, but coping—really coping, so that you deal with what *is* instead of what you'd like to be, with the loss of ego due to a profound failure or a loss of love—strengthens you. Anything that brings you into reality, into the present moment, is valuable. Happiness usually takes us into our illusions: "Isn't this wonderful; I've got everything I thought I wanted." Nothing happens in that place except often the sense of sadness, of "Is this all there is?"

One of the characters I played on stage, Shirley Valentine, makes a big change in her life when she decides to say "yes" to life. That's a big clue, saying "yes"; regarding life as an adventure, not always taking the safe way. It's important to say "yes" first, and then if it turns out that you were hasty, you can retract it. It's an important action to take. Actually, I've had to learn to say "no." I was never fearful; I was always anxious for the next adventure, but establishing my own boundaries was something I had to learn.

Since I turned fifty, I feel much more myself. I feel like I am who I've been becoming. Of course, I'm still becoming, but now I recognize who I am rather than feeling I'm not right and working toward something better. I hope I continue to grow and learn, but this is pretty much what I've got now. Certain things are okay with me now that weren't okay before—like my anger. I have a temper, and I was always trying to stamp it out, to achieve a calm, peaceful nature, sainthood if possible. I considered my anger a flaw. I've come to realize it is part and parcel of a wide emotional range. I don't just have anger; I have a large and deep reservoir of feelings that I work with. I can't just pluck out anger and keep all the other emotions. I wouldn't want to be less passionate or emotional. I've come to accept that my work uses all of my feelings: it comes from them, is the result of them. I don't fly off the handle as much as I used to. I can express my anger without being at the mercy of it. Self-acceptance is what I'm talking about. I don't feel I have to fulfill somebody else's concept of who I should be. Up until my fifties, I had a general feeling that there was a certain way to be and I wasn't it.

When I entered menopause, I was shocked because I realized we don't talk about it; everything was a surprise. I had no idea, for instance, that your lips get smaller. I'd never heard or read one word about that. But I kept noticing something different every time I put on my lipstick, and then I realized my lips were shrinking. I also had hot flashes for two years, which drove me nuts. I'm a very hot person anyway, I'm always hot. Everyone had told me there's nothing you can do about them. I went to see a wonderful lady doctor in Los Angeles about another problem, I asked her about hot flashes and she said, "Well, darling, when I was going through menopause and felt one coming on, I just said, 'No, I won't allow this' and I made them go away." I said, "Wait a minute, you're telling me you controlled hot flashes mentally?" She said, "I did." I couldn't wait for my next hot flash so I could make it go away with my thoughts, but I never got another one. It's one of the most miraculous events of my life: just by her telling me they could be controlled, they went away. Something clicked.

I don't know why I didn't take estrogen, I just allowed menopause to happen naturally, so I observed the whole process. Smaller lips was the worst because it's on my face and I make a living with my face. I did notice that men didn't seem as attractive as they used to—I mean they were nice looking, but I wasn't that interested. Last December I was in Memphis, Tennessee, and I had to go to an insurance doctor for the film I was doing. I told him of my concern about osteoporosis, because I've lost a quarter of an inch in my height in the last ten years, and that I'd been taking calcium but wasn't sure about how much to take. He asked if I was taking estrogen, and said that calcium needs estrogen in order to be metabolized. He gave me a videocassette tape called *Five Reasons Why Women Should Take Estrogen*. I watched the tape and it convinced me to take estrogen.

As soon as I started taking estrogen, I started having dreams about men! Suddenly, men were looking attractive. I said, "Wait a minute, this is a biochemical situation we've got going here!" Then I started getting my period again after not having one for twelve years. The first time I got one I was so shocked, I didn't say, "I got *my* period," I said, "I got *a* period." A friend of mine said, "Do you think there's some twenty-eight year old running around saying, 'Where's my period?'" The estrogen has also made my breasts fill out again. It's a very strange process; it's like time reversing itself—you go back to a more nubile stage. Women need to talk more about menopause. We aren't prepared for it.

Aging does make a difference in the roles I play. The film based on the play *The Cemetery Club* was great because it has several fine roles for older women, and we didn't have to have gray hair and dowdy ourselves down, which is often what happens. During the last few years, in the roles I've played on television, I've had to look like "their" idea of what a woman my age looks like, so I wasn't allowed to look like I actually look. In this film we're all allowed to appear as good as we can—that's so rare and so much fun. We're playing our ages with care. In Hollywood the roles are either for young girls, or thirty-year-old women, maybe forty; but once you get to fifty, it's grandmas. We don't have the kind of opportunities we had before. That's a drag. My profession is not like writing or photography or painting, where you just keep getting better at your craft. You do get better, but your piano gets creaky. You can play as well as you ever did—or better—but the piano legs wobble.

I'm interested to see if *The Cemetery Club* has any effect on my film career, because the last few roles I played, I portrayed a seventy year old. In *Mrs. Lambert Remembers Love,* with Walter Matthau, I was sixty-eight. I was originally seventy in the script, but I said, "Sixty-eight is old enough, thank you very much." It's fun to move forward in time, as long as you also get to move back in time. What happens is that you get stuck. People say, "Oh, I saw her in that show and she's so old."

My definition of success is that everybody who is making a movie thinks of *you* first for the part and sends you the scripts first, like Meryl Streep now. She has her pick of all the scripts that are written, and whatever she doesn't want gets sent out to the next level, and what *they* don't want goes to the next level; so success is getting first choice of all the work. The reward for good work is more work.

Success really wants to inflate you, and you have to get a hold of yourself. It's why I wouldn't go to the Oscars when I won; I knew I was going to win that night, but I didn't want to get sucked into the vortex. A few years went by, and after I lost the Oscar a few times, I thought, "I should have gone the first time; what's the matter with me?" As if there wasn't going to be some balance—life deals you enough blows, you don't have to stay out of the way of the blessings. At the time I had a great fear of inflation. As it turned out, life would have taken care of it for me, but I didn't know that then, so I pulled back from all the fanfare of success.

Fame comes with success in my business, but it's not necessarily success; fame is sort of an annoying byproduct, although to be perfectly honest, I only felt that way when I was the most sought after. After a while, when the attention receded a little, I missed it. I used to think, "Oh dear, all these people bothering me," and then when they stopped it was, "Where'd they go?" But all that's part of the leveling.

If actors ask me for advice about acting, I tell them, "The way to learn about acting is to act. You can't learn about it by getting a job, you have to join a group, a class or workshop where you're working together with other actors. You have to be really good if you're going to base your whole life on acting, because it's all about employment. With acting there's a theater and an audience, and people have to come to see you perform." I was very fortunate to find my way to Lee Strasberg, who was one of the great teachers of this century. He was responsible for my whole deepening process as a person. When I first went to him, I was cute and trying to be cuter. Lee introduced me to a whole other level of being and work, to my own depths. He was my mentor. He did the same thing for many people: Marilyn Monroe, Paul Newman, Al Pacino, Bobby DeNiro, Ann Jackson, Eli Wallach, Sally Fields, Jane Fonda, Joanne Woodward, Geraldine Page. The great ones. He was the main influence in our lives and in our work. Lee was a true theater genius. He changed my life.

Another experience that has changed my life is motherhood. In fact, it's the most important part of my life. My son and I are very bonded. When people ask me what I'm most proud of in my life, I say, "That I brought up a healthy, happy human being." He is a beautiful person, very outgoing, charming, funny, and dear. He has wonderful energy. I spent the first seven years of his life communicating to him that he was loved. I poured every ounce of love I had in me, that I could channel from the universe, into him. Consequently, my son is a stable person who loves other people and is respectful of them.

I've been unmarried for twenty-two years. Solitude. Blessed solitude has become very important to me. I find that when I have a day alone, I just revel in it, indulge in it, bathe in it. It's the most incredible luxury. Someone asked me, "Don't you get lonely?" I said, "I *desire* loneliness." That was not true before. Not that I ever had any time alone; I was active with husbands, boyfriends, sweethearts, son, etc. Now to take a walk by the river by myself, or sit and write, or stare into the fire is so wonderful. That seems to come with the fifties.

I look forward to the crone. I think that's the great gift that is the balancing force for all the things we give up by aging. What we get in return is the Wise Woman. I'm looking forward to her.

CLAIRE
BRAZ-VALENTINE

*My fantasy of aging is to age well enough so that younger women would
think,* Gee, I wish I were her age. *I want the stigma of aging to be removed from women. So, for all those younger women and for myself, I intend to do it with as much panache as I can. I'm going to put everything
I've got into it.*

profile

THE LAST WILL AND TESTAMENT OF THIS WOMAN

To every woman who is my daughter
To every woman who is my sister:

I will to you first of all, my diets—
my grapefruit diet, my orange diet, rice diet, wine diet, water diet,
banana diet and fasting diet.

I will you every time anyone ever said to me, "Have you ever
thought of going on a diet?"

I will you TOPS clubs, Weight Watchers Clubs, Pill Pushing
Doctors, amphetamines, water pills, thyroid pills, and laxatives
   that I have known
and I have known many—

I will you all the times I wished the scale would say 125 instead of 145

I will you a living girdle,
an eighteen hour girdle,
a four way stretch girdle,
a two way stretch girdle.
an I can't believe it's a girdle girdle,
a rubber girdle full of holes that "breathed" when I couldn't.
a girdle with legs so tight I left it in the public bathroom in the waste-
basket—
a garbage can full of girdles,
And the day a man told me, "You got an ass that could kill a man"
And all the time it was killing me.

I will you my bras,
my bra with under-wires that pushed me up,
my cross-my-heart bra that pushed me out,
my padded bras that made me fuller,
my natural bras that made me natural,
a garbage can full of bras—
a dresser full of bras—
and the everlasting indecision about whether to or not to.

I will you something called a Merry Widow
which is something like an iron maiden.
I will you all the tears I cried lying on the bed at six o'clock in
the morning after my junior prom,
trapped in the damn thing
till I thought I was squeezed to death
And my mother finally freeing my tortured body.

I will you my diaphragm that didn't fit,
that got stuck,
that got a hole in it,
that slipped,
that I forgot and wore for a week.
I will you my diaphragm pregnancy.

I will you my coil that made me bleed every day for a year.
I will you my bow that made me bleed every day for three months.
I will you my pregnancy that I lost because I bled so much.

I will you my birth control pills
that made me throw up,
grew me big breasts
and then spots on my face
and a terrible case of nervousness
and a good start on a beard.

I will you my douche bag
filled with lemon flavored scents,
mint flavored scents,
flower flavored scents,
washed rinsed and flushed with flavored scents.

I will you all the foams and jellies and sprays
and suppositories that I was ever
tempted to insert into that most mysterious warehouse of undesirable
smell.
I give you them all.
I give you them all.

I give you my false eyelashes
false fingernails
my perfume
my pancake makeup
my blusher
my rouge
my eye shadow
my mascara that made my eyes bigger,
that made my eyes darker,

that made my eyes like a distorted clown
when I cried.

I give you every ad I ever read
that made me think I needed these things.

I will to you every bit of shame I ever was made to feel
about being the woman I was born to be.

I will you all of this
in the hopes that once you have all these things
you will realize that you don't need them
much sooner than I realized that.

CLAIRE BRAZ-VALENTINE

THE TRUTH CAN BE FUNNY, AND IT CAN ALSO HURT: Claire Braz-Valentine offers the gift of truth in her writing. I first met Claire at a women's circle, where she read the above poem—at once a tribute to and a confession of what women endure in order to fit society's idea of "beautiful" and be anything but what they truly are. I was captivated by the air of mystery a black hat and dark glasses gave her. I was enchanted by her talent and the way in which her words took command of my psyche, offering me an emotional roller-coaster ride: from laughing hysterically to verging on tears because I recognized myself in them.

Later, she read an excerpt from a play she had recently finished writing on Amelia Earhart, the first woman to make a solo flight across the Atlantic, and who disappeared under mysterious circumstances near New Guinea in 1937. I was simply dazzled by the rhythm and spin of her words, which are spoken by a flying Amelia in a monologue. I heard the determination and unabashed feminist stance of a woman who refused to live a life that was expected of her or one that was confined in any way. A week later, during our first interview, I realized those words applied not only to Amelia, but to Claire as well.

Claire was born and raised in San Francisco. Her father was the son of Portuguese immigrants from the Azores, and her mother was the daughter of Irish immigrants who came through Ellis Island. She attended an all-girl's Catholic school, and credits the attending nuns with imbuing her with a sense of confidence in herself that has rarely swayed.

Married at nineteen, Claire gave birth to three sons in rapid succession and then found herself raising them alone as a single mother. A short story was her first publication, followed by several poems in various magazines. Living in Santa Cruz, California, she became an administrator at the University of California in the literature department, advising graduate students in the program. Twelve years ago, through a set of serendipitous circumstances, Claire was invited to write a play for the Bear Republic Theatre.

When the actors in her play, *Embrace Tiger, Return to Mountain,* walked out on the stage and began to speak the words she had written, Claire knew that she had "*finally found* it. I was home!" She thanked God and the Muses for the discovery of the new direction her life would take: that of a feminist playwright.

Browsing in a bookstore a few months later, Claire pulled from the shelf a diary that had been written by a pioneer woman living on the prairie in Wyoming in the 1800s. An entry made sometime during the 1860s describes a historic and unforgettable incident: the country woman, seeing a wagon circled by a cloud of dust on the horizon, sat in her rocking chair on the porch—a shotgun across her lap, her children standing behind her—waiting for the arrival of the unrecognized wagon. When it pulled up in front of her house, a woman stepped down, walked to the porch, stretched out her hand, and said, "Hello, my name is Susan B. Anthony. I'm having a meeting for women in town next week and I want you to come."

Claire spent the next two years researching and writing a play based on the life of Susan B. Anthony. Her play, *This One Thing I Do,* was so successful that it was purchased by publisher Samuel P. French and staged in New York off-Broadway. It reenacts Anthony's fifty-year friendship with Elizabeth Cady Stanton and their tireless fight for women's rights. Claire's purpose in her plays is to remind us that women *have* gone before us, that women *have* succeeded, "that women *have* worked for you and me."

A third play, *When Will I Dance,* about the outwardly flamboyant but inwardly tormented life of Mexican artist Frida Kahlo, came next. It too was staged in New York and received an enthusiastic response.

That day when I first met her, Claire also read a poem she had written to "my guys" as well as a few pieces written by them. Her "guys" turned out to be inmates of Soledad State Penitentiary—she was their teacher and friend in the creative writing program there. In response to my request to accompany Claire to one of her biweekly writer's groups, she arranged for me to spend a Saturday afternoon in a room with twenty men inside a maximum security prison—or a correctional facility, as it is euphemistically called.

Claire admits, "Generally, if somebody doesn't understand why I teach at Soledad, there is no way to explain it to them. If they haven't met these men, they could never know what they mean to me and how much I learn from them."

The level of support, enthusiasm, camaraderie, and genuine interest the men showed toward each other's writing was affecting, and the quality of the work impressive. I learned a great deal about Claire through the eyes of her students, about her commitment, her vision, her loyalty. One man told me, "Claire's got heart. And heart in here has a whole different connotation than it does on the outside—

heart in here is a small man who stands up to a big one; heart in here is the guy who keeps going day after day when he feels like he could fall through the floor; heart in here is the guy who walks to the weight pile every day just to keep himself going—it's a whole different meaning. Claire's got heart." Another one said, "Even when the institution's locked down, she will sit in this room alone for two or three hours—nothing can drag her away—until we're clear to come to class. Yet this doesn't discourage her." Her students—Sarge, Terry, Craig, Dave, Mohammed, Manny, Frazer, Howard, Paul, and others—all spoke to me about Claire's humanity, which she often expresses through her unfailing sense of humor. As another student said with a smile, "We hear she has a great right hook!"

I began to understand why Claire told me, during our drive to Soledad, that the year she had been teaching there was one of the most important in her life; why a single woman in her fifties—recently retired from an administrative position at the University of California, Santa Cruz, the mother of three grown sons, a radical feminist, a published poet, and an acclaimed playwright—was willing to give up "two whole days every other week." But I wouldn't have known the answer unless I'd experienced it myself. I wouldn't have understood until I saw Claire in a room filled with prison inmates and heard her say, "We are writers, nothing else matters."

I TURNED FIFTY VERY SHORTLY AFTER *When Will I Dance,* my play on Frida Kahlo, opened. My youngest son had just graduated from college. It wasn't easy raising three sons as a divorced mother. I had been working as an administrator at the University of California, Santa Cruz, for fifteen years. Sometimes blending motherhood, my writing, and a full-time job took its toll on me. I had three spinal surgeries within five years. I pushed myself too hard and my body was falling apart. That's why Frida first appealed to me: she'd had twenty-seven spinal surgeries. I identified with her and with her pain, and I began writing the play on her while I was recuperating. I was still wearing a brace. I wrote sometimes on my back in bed.

Writing that play was one of the hardest things I've ever done. I had to figure out how to keep her from being overshadowed by all the people who went through her life the way she had been in real life. So I began taking them out one by one: Henry Ford, Trotsky, all the celebrities. Finally, I was down to Diego and Frida and I thought, "Phooey, you're going, too, Diego." So I offed him. But I knew I didn't want to write a one-woman play. I had Frida posters all over the house. One day I said, "Okay, Frida, you win." I thought I had been beaten; I thought she did not want me to write about her.

This sounds dramatic, but it is the truth. The last day—by this time, I had a little computer—I was going to shut the computer off, and I picked up a book and read an entry from her diary about how she saw herself in the reflection of a window when she was six years old and had polio. She drew a little circle on the glass and went through it. There she saw the other Frida dancing for her— she imagined herself whole. It was as if the door had opened for me as well. This was Frida's other self, and when I looked again at her paintings, it was all there. So I wrote the play with two Fridas and called it *When Will I Dance,* which is what I imagined her asking the child she had imagined. It was magic. I never explained why there were two. Sometimes they could see each other, sometimes not. They interact and support and help each other, destroy and nurture each other. I knew that was the play for Frida; I just had to be patient long enough for it to come to me.

After this play opened in New York, the university lowered the retirement age to fifty. Within a week I had my retirement papers, and I left shortly after that. No one could believe I was really going to go. I could hardly believe it. I no longer needed to take care of three little boys. When I was a little girl, I had two goals: to be a mother and to be a writer. I had done mothering and loved it. Now was my chance to be a writer. Money has never been terribly important to me. Everything I earned during all the years my sons were young went into just staying alive, providing a home, and as good a life for them as I could. I never took a vacation. I drove an old car. I bought most of my clothes at thrift shops. I figured if I stayed at the job and got used to having all that money just for myself, that I would never live my dream of being a full-time writer. I held onto the dream. It felt like I was putting my foot on a high wire and stepping out, but I knew that if I fell, I fell alone and I would just have to get up.

That first year after my retirement I started giving private writing work-shops. I really enjoyed it. I loved to write and it showed. All those years of staying up late at night after work, after the boys were sleeping, putting down one more line on paper, had given me the experience I needed for this next phase of my life.

I futzed around that first year, trying to figure out what to write. It was difficult finding my own rhythm, after leading such a full life with children and a demanding job. My plays on Susan B. Anthony and Frida Kahlo were doing well. There was definitely a pattern emerging. I like writing about women in history. Every time I "discovered" another woman in history, I became so fascinated with her that I needed to write about her just to get her out of my system. I have always said that characters come out of history to live in my bathtub until I write about them. They nag me night and day until I write about them. Then they get out and leave me alone to bathe in peace.

About that time I read a book on Amelia Earhart that was a piece of fluff— it only skimmed the surface of her life, and made her seem like a spoiled woman, which is not at all what she was. I read several more books on her and discovered that she was an amazing woman. Then, lo and behold, I got into the shower one morning and there she was, waiting for her voice, wanting me to tell her story. I was hooked. And last Thursday I finished her play, it's called *Blue Skies Forever.*

I have remained single for many years now. Who knows? Maybe tomorrow I'll meet a person I want to be in relationship with. I'm completely open to that possibility and it would be wonderful. However, the one thing I'm very careful about is that I do not become a woman whose obsession is to couple up, to find identity through someone else, to be so male-identified that she has no identity herself.

Let me put it this way. When I was in the fourth grade, one of the nuns gave us a wonderful piece of wisdom: "When each of you comes into the world, you are given a bucket. And when you leave this world, regardless of whether your bucket is small, medium-sized, or very, very huge, God checks that bucket. And it must be filled to the top. Each of you knows how big your bucket is and what you must do to fill it. Never, never forget it. That is your mission." She felt that we'd been given that wisdom somewhere in us, and I've been very conscious of that.

So, who wouldn't love to fall in love? I love being in love, but I know that my mission is to complete this body of work and I'm obsessed with that. I love my work. Yes, I could walk into the delicatessen tomorrow to buy a loaf of French bread and meet someone. My whole life could be upside down for six months, and then after those six months, I hope I'm back in the library and also have a nice relationship. At some point, when I was younger, it had a lot more importance.

I guess my fantasy of aging is to age well enough so that younger women would think, *Gee, I wish I were her age*. I want to do it well, because I feel that women who do things well inspire younger women to do them. I want the stigma of aging to be removed from women. So, for all those younger women and for myself, I intend to do it with as much panache as I can. I'm going to put *everything* I've got into it.

About ten years ago, I was asked if I would serve as a judge on a panel for the prisoners' literary contest at Soledad. When I volunteered as a judge for the annual contest, I always thought I would like to work in the prison, to work with women and help give them a sense of themselves. That was my vision.

Then two years ago, when I told the William James Association [an organization that puts artists in prisons to teach] I was retiring from the university, they said that the writing teacher at Soledad was also retiring and that I'd be perfect for the job. I said I'd love to, and then I remembered they were men, *big* men. This was scary; it was not what I had in mind. But I realized that all of the really interesting things we do in life are not always quite what we had in mind, and if we surprise ourselves a little bit, yay for us!

The first time I walked into that room on my own I was nervous. At that time the class had about fifteen men. I read some of my work so they could hear what I'd done, and we began one of the most meaningful relationships of my life. I have learned so much about myself in the year I've been working there. I have learned about patience, control, loyalty, confidentiality, friendship, and trust. I have learned about a freedom of spirit and determination that I had never had any concept existed. In fact, my new play on Amelia Earhart is dedicated to them. I love what I'm doing; I love the men I work with, and I know the feeling is entirely mutual. I don't mean that I love them like my children; I love them as writers, they are struggling so hard to find themselves. I work very hard for them—I take home stacks of their manuscripts to read—and I work them very hard.

The frustrating part about working in a prison is that at any time a transfer can come up, and they're gone to another prison or another unit in the prison where they won't allow instructors. You see them one week, and the next week you will never see them again. And you don't even know they're going. The class goes through a mourning period. We miss them terribly when they're gone.

When they are in the room with me, we shut the door and this is our special time. We are writers. Everything else goes away. I forget where I am and they forget where they are, thank God. I'm made to wear an alarm box, and if something happens, I'm supposed to press the box. I tease them sometimes and say, "If you read me a bad poem, I'll press the alarm." They say the box is to protect them from my critique—if I get too tough, they'll press the alarm to have themselves removed. It is a wonderful gift for me to be able to do this work. I do get paid, even though I put more time in than I get paid for.

There are twenty-four correctional institutions in California that compete in a statewide contest for twenty prizes in writing (I no longer am a judge), and my students took *ten* of them. When I first came into the class, I said, "Hey, I know I have a soft look and I'm fun and that we have a good time and that you're used to having a man in here. I understand this. But," I said, "I want to make something really clear: I am extremely competitive. Therefore you are going to *win* this contest, you are going to *sweep* the prizes. Do you understand? You are going to rewrite and rewrite and *rewrite* until you get it right. You are going to work hard and be proud that you are winners. That means I'm going to be a winner, and that's what I want." They said, "Yes, ma'am; yes, ma'am." And by gosh they did it!

I was so very, very proud of them. We are really very close. It's hard for people to understand this. There are certain members of my family—not my sons—who simply don't talk much about the fact that I work with male felons, because if they did, they would have to hear that these men might be murderers or rapists—they're not in there for parking tickets (maybe some are, but I don't think so), and it's too frightening for them. But it's not frightening to me at all.

It's not important to me why they are in prison. I'm encouraged, as an instructor, to read their files, to find out why each person is there. I've done it on a few occasions, but it doesn't seem to make any difference to me at all. That part of their life is irrelevant to what we do in class. Although it's hard to work with somebody's writing and not know them—everything comes out eventually, anyway.

Sometimes, people ask me how I, as a feminist, could work in a prison with men who may have never given much thought to women's rights. Let's face it, some of them are in there because of crimes against women. I simply ask them in return, "Who would you suggest we send in there, someone who's very concerned about women's issues, or someone who doesn't give a darn?" Anyway, most of the guys I work with are happy to find a strong woman. I find that most of them have learned to judge people by how they act, not by their gender.

Somehow, I need to find a way eventually to work with parolees. We pop people out into society after prison, and most people have no *concept* of what is happening in prisons and to those lives when they get out. Most of those men are all coming back out; they are all going to be in your life and my life. I work with writers in prison who want to write after they are released; often they are without funds, without support of family or friends. I would love to find a way to work with them. I would also like to work in a women's prison, to do both. Unless they force me out, I couldn't give up the men's prison.

There's so much to fill my bucket with; my bucket is only one-quarter full. I have a lot of work to do, but I'm going to enjoy it immensely. These middle years are the years during which I will fill it. The groundwork, which is my children, my family, has been laid. Now, I feel I'm just hitting my working years, my creative years—these are the days!

DEANNE BURKE

When I think about what it means to be fifty, I ask myself, Should there be leisure time in all this? I think there should be. Here I am in the pausal time of my life—the physiological pausal time. A pause means rest to me, but I don't see rest at this time.

profile

49 is divine
50 is nifty
51 is when you start shopping at Thrifty

JON BURKE

DEANNE BURKE WAS SO PROUD OF HER SON and the above haiku-like poem he had written for her on her birthday last year that she delightedly shared it with me. Jonathan is twelve years old and Deanne is now fifty-two. She views the prospect of reexperiencing adolescence in her fifties through her son as a "challenge." But probably no more challenging than when, at the age of thirty-nine, she discovered she was pregnant. "I felt it was a white light that had come to me," she says, and made the decision ("I didn't consider abortion") to assume the full responsibility for raising her child as a single parent. Anyone who spends even a brief amount of time with them can clearly see that the devotion between Deanne—"Jonathan is my priority"—and her son—"Isn't my mom beautiful!"—is mutual.

For this interview I met with Deanne one Saturday afternoon. Instead of the three hours we had planned, we spent eight hours reminiscing, through tears and laughter and pizza, about our fourteen-year friendship. It was a lovely spring day, and the plum trees throughout Berkeley were in full flower—the blossoms mirroring the color of playful children's ruddy cheeks. We finally settled comfortably in the living room, after first trying the back deck (it was too hot), the spare bedroom (there was no back support on the bed), and the kitchen (it was too cool).

Jonathan and his friends, who had been watching a football game on the television in the living room, decided to shoot a few hoops downstairs in the driveway. In between frequent interruptions from several spirited preteen boys ("Are you finished yet?" "How long will it take?" "Can we watch television now?" "Why are you taking photographs?" "We're starving! Can we order a pizza?" "Can Robert stay all night?"), two high-strung dogs—Peaches, hers; Sienna, mine—tussling over territory and a tyrannized cat, an impertinent telephone, an intrusive doorbell and clamorous rock and roll, we managed to secure a few intermittent periods of quiet. Is it any wonder that Deanne's fantasy of aging is: QUIET?!

"This is what my life is like," she said, without a hint of regret or martyrdom. We spoke about menopause and the irony that during this "pausal time" in her life there was definitely *no pause* to be found. She spoke frankly and revealingly about what it's like to be a single mom, her sex life, our collective accountability for the homeless, the death of her dearest and oldest male friend, the responsibility inherent in teaching grade-school children, dealing with ailing parents, buying a house on a teacher's salary, and her vision of aging.

Many years ago, when Jonathan was still a baby, Deanne and her son spent a blissful summer in the high desert near Bishop, California. As she described what this experience had meant to her, I couldn't help but make an analogy between her impression of the desert and her personal life. "I see the desert as a real utilitarian place, and that's how I see my life, I suppose. There is such a perfect ecosystem—it's all so interrelated. I was thinking about the saguaro cactus, how every part of it is integral. It is slow growing but lives two hundred years, weighs two tons, and gets to be fifty feet high. Many animals use it, the elf owl and doves and bats pollinate the flowers; some cultures use the fruit. Finally, when it dies, it decomposes and other animals inhabit it.

"I think of the desert as so sparse, and yet it's rich. It's efficient. It's quiet!" she laughed calmly, in response to a new ruckus from the dogs.

The saguaro cactus looks human: its arms reach out and up, as if welcoming you or praying to a cactus god in the sky. It has its own system of moisture, which you could think of as a bloodstream. Yes, I could see how Deanne could so completely identify with this noble cactus, how the ecology of that plant is a metaphor for a human life, with every aspect—son, work, home, parents, lover, friends, and social responsibility—forming a beautiful kind of interdependence. But one must distinguish between living, which is busy and full of desires, and being, which is quiet. And so I understood when she exclaimed, "I think I'm going to be a saguaro in my next life!"

ROM THE TIME I WAS IN MY EARLY TWENTIES, I knew I wanted to have a child. I was torn between being a person of my generation who was born in the '40s, and an independent woman emerging in the '60s. I read Simone de Beauvoir and Betty Friedan and became stronger; their writings opened up a whole other avenue of possibility for me. Certainly, the women who evolved through the women's movement during the '60s and '70s are stronger for having experienced some of the freedoms that the women's movement fought for—including abortions. We just didn't have that option available to us when we were in our late teens and early twenties.

I was married in my early twenties to a young man my age whom I had known since junior high and high school. He wasn't interested in having children because he felt he had a lot to explore in the world first. We traveled together and spent nearly a year in Bulgaria, the Soviet Union, East Germany, and Hungary.

My ex-husband was involved in student politics at the University of California at Berkeley. I moved to Berkeley because he convinced me that "this is *the* place to be right now." This was in 1960: Caryl Chessman was in San Quentin, Kennedy was elected, the Civil Rights Movement was active. We were very involved in civil rights and participated in anti–House Un-American Activities Committee demonstrations. Berkeley was a groundswell of student foment and fervency. *That* was our baby. It was only after we separated that I began to realize how much I wanted a child, but it didn't happen for a long time.

For years I had tried to conceive with a man who had been my lover, but was unable. And then at the age of thirty-nine, I conceived. I felt it was a white light that had come to me and there was no turning back. I didn't consider abortion—I knew this child was meant to be. I made the decision based on the fact that I would raise Jonathan myself—regardless of whether his father would be supportive or not—and assume the sole financial responsibility. To Jonathan's good fortune, once he was born and grew beyond infancy, his dad turned out to be there for him. He was not an emotional support for me, but I was never asking for that. There was an unexpected surging and welling of family support, even though I would be an older parent and didn't know exactly how I was going to manage financially. It all worked out.

His father already had two daughters from a wife that he was separated from but not yet divorced. It turned out to be an unusual satellite family for Jonathan. His stepmother grew to open her heart to this situation, and continues to have

Christmas at her house with all three kids—sometimes I participate. Jonathan feels that this is his family. It's what we call the "diversity of family," and I think it's given Jonathan a lot of strength and security. So, in a sense, I'm grateful to Jonathan's father for offering this situation.

The two most intimate experiences of my lifetime have been giving birth and being part of someone's death—seeing the full circle. I do feel that making love is intimate, but you can make love over and over again. You can also give birth a number of times, but you can't give birth to that same person, and you can't go a second chance with someone's death—that's one experience of a lifetime.

Having a child and being a single parent has opened my heart in a way that I don't believe anything else could have done. The whole rush of feelings from a love for your child that is so forgiving, so full. Experiencing your own child: taking care of that small human form, watching them reach their milestones. There's nothing else in life like that, although you can watch other people's children and be part of another family. The love for your child is an eternal, unconditional love. Having had my own child has made me a better person, I think. I'm more open, more giving, more forgiving. It's probably made me a better teacher—more compassionate and empathetic.

It's such a mark to turn fifty: you can look back, you can look forward. You look back at the light and the dark; you look forward to the light and you know there will certainly be more darkness. I see it all as the full cycle of life. Perhaps that's because my parents are still alive, even though they are in a state of health that renders them frail. I'm looking at both ends: an emerging adolescent full of wonder, curiosity, energy, and hope, and aging parents who wake every morning and *want* to be hopeful, but the lack of good health makes them see that the end is near.

Raising Jonathan has made me more compassionate toward my parents. I'm a good mother to them now, a patient and understanding mother. I see their vulnerability and frailty; how hard it is for them to manage their lives. They are becoming less and less capable, so they look to me and to my brother. As Jonathan needs less help but more guidance, they need more help.

When I think about what it means to be fifty, I ask myself, "Should there be leisure time in all this?" I think there should be. Here I am in the pausal time of my life—the physiological pausal time, not in the practical, day-to-day living. A pause means rest to me, but I don't see rest at this time. I teach full time and make high demands on myself. Because after twenty-five years I have become a veteran teacher, I'm always looking at new ways to teach, new areas to learn about—I want to stay informed. So many new issues have arisen: environmental and social. Teaching about Native Americans and African Americans has definitely changed. How do you best introduce children to think about

Columbus differently, about who was in North America first? What have we as Europeans done to this land? I want to teach the truthful facts about slavery and civil rights in this country.

It's important to bring good literature into the classroom that children *want* to read. We're living in a technological society where you have Nintendos and computers that are much more attractive to children than books. But you want them to be actively involved with other stories that aren't being passively televised on a screen. I've discovered that I need to recapture my students' interest through picture books once again.

I wonder why young people at universities and young working people are not more politically involved when there's so much that needs to be done. I don't see any concerted effort, as a movement, to do anything about the homeless, which I think is a real class issue. Maybe it's because the people who are homeless are so disenfranchised, they have no connections; whereas the Vietnam War crossed the class structure—boys were drafted from the working class, the middle class, and a few from the privileged classes. It's hard to know why more isn't being done. Homelessness is increasing and it's in every city across the United States.

Still, I have hope. I listened to Helen Caldecott—she's an optimistic person, but also very practical. She offers us a new direction and some alternatives—if we would only take them—for saving the Earth. We need to do something, and my hope is that enough people will be concerned so that we will all do something in unison.

I came from a tight family in Cleveland. We moved en masse with aunts, uncles, and a grandfather to Los Angeles when I was four and a half. What I remember is being in a close-knit family with good values, including respect for the older generation. My grandfather lived with us for years. So, as an adult, I have kept some of those basic values: respect for people and respect for work. I remember how my mother took care of her best friend who, at the age of thirty-six, had breast cancer. She lived with us until the last three weeks of her life, at which time my father and her husband drove her to her mother's house. That experience made such a deep impression on me. I learned that friends and family are there to help one another, and whatever the issues may be, you stick by one another.

Menopause has been a fairly easy transition for me. I've actually been in the staging area of it for the last four years. There are a variety of inconveniences or physical discomforts. I do experience some of the typical symptoms—the night sweats, the occasional rush of anxiety in a large setting (a department store or subway or just large crowds), vaginal dryness—but it's manageable and it hasn't caused me to feel like I can't do anything I have been able to do in the past. I notice that my skin is drier and I've got sun spots. One night I'll go to bed, and

I'll wake up the next morning with something different on my body—a new mole or more gray hair. Definite changes happen. The expression "the change of life" is accurate, but the changes can also be welcoming.

Currently, I'm in the dilemma of trying to make a decision about hormone replacement. I read all the statistics in the women's magazines and medical magazines. It's supposed to help with replenishment and prevent osteoporosis and heart disease, but you are also putting something foreign into your body. The issue is a dilemma for women in their fifties because the medical profession is recommending it. Women used to take hormones without even thinking; now there's a conscious debate. How do you choose? I'm still thinking about it.

There was a long period of time after Jonathan was born when I was without a man. But I felt fulfilled; it was fine. I didn't feel the need to be living with a man or even to be sexually involved. I was alone for seven years, and then last year an old friendship was renewed. Through the shared experience of two deaths in three years, we were brought even closer and we provided support for each other. Up until we began seeing each other, I was certain I would spend the rest of my life alone. He is wonderful to Jonathan and my parents.

How does it feel to still be a woman with sexual desires and be menopausal? There are times when I fully enjoy being with a man as a lover, and there are times when I don't feel so driven. Either I'm tired, or I'm doing something that's taking my time so fully, like work or creating something or being with my son. Most important for me, whether I would be menopausal or not, is building memories with people, forming ties.

Nearly three years ago I lost a very close friend with whom I'd continued a friendship and been lovers with for over twenty-five years. He provided such a sense of security for me—not financial, but personal, emotional. He encouraged me in everything I did, and was truly one of those human beings who seldom come into one's life. I spent the last six months of his life with him, before he died from esophageal cancer—on Jonathan's birthday, November 18. Every year Jonathan asks me, "Do you think Bob did that on purpose?" I tell him, "Of course he did. He never wants us to forget him." It will always be a reminder, a happy reminder.

Bob was so encouraging. I felt his encouragement during my pregnancy with Jonathan, during the Caesarean birth, and afterwards at home. He was there at the hospital photographing me, and bought things that I needed when I came home. We never married, yet we shared something so intimate—we shared his death. It was so peaceful. He died in his own house with people he loved surrounding him and good books, good music. He was still looking for kindred spirits.

Since the time Jonathan was born, I've taught full time and saved enough money to put a down payment on a house. Four years ago I entered a business arrangement called "tenant-in-common," in which I bought a duplex with another woman who is divorced and has two children. We met through a mutual friend of ours. We don't rely on one another for emotional support, nor do we exchange sitting arrangements. There was no other prearranged goal for us except to buy this duplex. It has worked out, and I think it *can* work for people.

I had one non-interest loan from a close friend, which I had to repay within two years. The rest I saved. I was fortunate to have lived in a flat for nearly sixteen years in which the rent was so modest. For the first three years, I had people renting a room in my duplex; but last year I decided to keep it vacant. Financially, I've been able to do it, but it's a sacrifice knowing that I have a thirty-year mortgage and a balloon payment after fifteen years. I don't know when I'm going to retire—I hope I won't be working until I'm eighty! But I don't feel compulsive about it.

Although I don't quite identify with the concept of owning my own house, I bought it for good reasons. It wasn't that I needed to own property because it would give me a sense of power. I did it because I knew rentals were only going to increase, and I needed to have some control over my life; one way was to own a place where the mortgage wouldn't increase as rentals do. It would stay a fixed amount. We still go on vacations, but the first couple of years were really meager.

For the longest time, I got hand-me-down clothes for Jonathan and they were perfect. I'd shop at secondhand stores. My arrangement with his father is that we would each pay Jonathan's expenses when he was with either one of us. I think Jonathan knows he is being influenced by the media in terms of consumerism. He is a sensitive person and understands that his father is a retired longshoreman with a fixed income who has three kids. But some of his friends have their own telephones and very generous clothing allowances. I'm talking about twelve-year-old children who are in their first year of junior high.

In some ways I think Jonathan is a stronger person for having a mother who works full time and who is pretty strict about ethics and values and beliefs. He constantly invites his friends over, so obviously he feels okay about where we live and who I am. He's not ashamed of or embarrassed by me. That makes me feel good because there are many kids his age who are already embarrassed by their families; it's a shame. I don't know what Jonathan will tell me ten years from now about my having made the decision to raise him as a single parent. At this point he doesn't think of it as a selfish choice. I'm hoping he'll understand why I made the choice to have him. He certainly is a wonderful person as I see him growing and developing, and I'm proud of who he is and how he thinks about and views life. He has a wide range of friends. I've never heard him say, "I've got this unusual family," or, "Why did you do this?"

My father is eighty-six and my mother is eighty-three, so I probably will live until ninety. What would I like to do between now and ninety? I'd like to see Machu Picchu and the Amazon area. I'd like to travel and to really get to know the desert better.

I don't think I would change the color of my hair, although a friend of mine said, "You can take the girl out of Los Angeles, but you can't take Los Angeles out of the girl." I like wearing lipstick. Is that because I grew up close to Hollywood? I don't know. I think it's fun. I can't imagine having a face-lift or ever doing anything surgical to my body that's unnecessary, and I don't think that's necessary. I look forward to becoming older; I like it. There's nothing about aging that I don't like so far. Even gravity hasn't bothered me yet!

When I look at some women and I see how life is written all over them, I think, "Isn't that wonderful." I don't see it as frightening at all. What's most important to me is to continue to learn, to be curious, to find out about new things. I don't care about gravity pulling me down or a sagging breast or cellulite. It's definitely seeing a new play, hearing some new music, reading a new poem, experiencing social change—those are the things that are important to me.

CHARLAYNE HUNTER-GAULT

It's very important to have another woman friend or friends who are the same age or just a little older . . . Let's face it, not all women in their fifties are healthy or positive. We can help each other by sharing our own positive ideas and attitudes.

profile

"I believe in having a secret life with secret plans and secret dreams," says a slave mother to her daughter. "Just like having a little vegetable garden to yourself out back of your cabin like mine. You got to work it at night or real early in the morning, but it's yours. Same with dreams. Maybe you got to work them late at night or real early in the morning, but ain't nobody can take them out of your head lest they kill you, and if you work ain't nobody going to kill you, 'cause you too valuable."

BARBARA CHASE-RIBOUD, *Sally Hemings*

CHARLAYNE HUNTER-GAULT'S SECRET LIFE BEGAN as a twelve-year-old living in Atlanta, Georgia, when she dreamed of a future as a journalist. "A beautiful white woman with red hair and blue eyes"—comic-strip character Brenda Starr—was her unlikely role model. This "beautiful woman" was an unlikely role model not only because she was a fictional comic-strip character, but because as an African American in the segregated South, Charlayne knew the difficulties inherent in a prejudiced world. Even her high school counselor tried to discourage her by bringing her "down to the reality of my life's chances."

At sixteen Charlayne took her first big step in making her dream come true by applying to the University of Georgia's School of Journalism. The university had never admitted a black applicant in its 175-year history, and for two years her fantasy was deferred. But in 1961, undaunted by the obstacles and "inspired by the support of people of good will," she was finally admitted (along with Hamilton Holmes) to the University of Georgia. Although she walked alone through the jeers and taunts (and even tear gas from the riots outside her dormitory) protesting her presence, which had been ordered by the federal court, she was not alone. "Knowing that," she says, "gave me the courage to continue that journey."

Three decades later Charlayne has become an "evening star" (or a "Media Goddess," as a plaque in her office proclaims) as a broadcast journalist. Since 1978 she has held the position of correspondent and substitute anchor on the "MacNeil/Lehrer News Hour" on PBS and has garnered an impressive array of accolades, including two National News and Documentary Emmy Awards, the Newswomen's Club of New York Front Page Award, the American Women in Radio and Television Award, the Women of Achievement Award, two Public

Broadcasting System Awards, and the Peabody Award in 1986 for "Apartheid's People," a five-part series on South Africa.

Her office in the WNET building in midtown Manhattan is large but crammed with memorabilia, photographs, books, plaques, awards, and framed letters from admiring fans. As I waited there for Charlayne, I was reminded of something Isaac Bashevis Singer once said when his wife asked him how he could work in such a cluttered study: "In the beginning was chaos." On the day of our meeting, there was ample time to browse, as I had an unexpected period of over an hour waiting for Charlayne to return from her foray into a local state prison to tape an upcoming segment for "MacNeil/Lehrer." My consolation prize turned out to be meeting Robin MacNeil, whose office is opposite Charlayne's. He was as personable and gracious as he appears to be every night on my television screen at six o'clock P.M.

At last Charlayne arrived in her office, snacking on a cup of frozen yogurt. She was even more attractive in person than she is on TV. Her brilliant green eyes stood out against her bronze skin and her iridescent cobalt blue jacket. I commented on her chic new hairstyle, and she told me that she loves to experiment with her hair.

Charlayne answered my questions and entered into an easy dialogue with the same direct and insightful approach she uses in her own interviewing process. I learned that she had only recently completed an autobiography called *In My Place,* a memoir of her experience at the University of Georgia in particular and of the Civil Rights Movement in general. She wrote it while working as a full-time national and foreign investigative reporter for "MacNeil/Lehrer," and while continuing to live her private life as a wife and the mother of two grown children.

That evening we watched the broadcast of a previously taped interview Charlayne had done with Wangari Matthai, a Kenyan environmentalist who is responsible for organizing women in her country to plant 10 million trees, and who that week was making a presentation at the 1992 Earth Summit in Rio de Janeiro. As I watched the program with Charlayne, I saw two beautiful, dynamic, powerful women contributing their skills to make a better world for everyone. I had two parts of her before me: the skilled interviewer on television, and the intelligent, articulate conversationalist discussing her own life with me.

And there was another side: that of the caring daughter. During the broadcast, she called her mother (who was up from Georgia and staying with Charlayne and her husband in their Manhattan apartment) to remind her of the showing of the Matthai interview. It was a comedy of errors as Charlayne patiently tried to explain to her mother just how to turn on the television set and find channel thirteen on the cable box. A confusing (for the mother) and frustrating (for the daughter) task.

She has been recognized as a serious and outstanding print and broadcast journalist. Her professional work on television provides a more positive frame of reference for minorities and women who watch the show. She has become a real-life alternative to the fictional Brenda Starr. It is understandable that women viewers throughout the country write to Charlayne to thank her for bringing a woman's compassionate perspective to the daily news, to coverage of the Gulf War, the Los Angeles riots, to race relations and women's issues. It is difficult to define what it means to women to have a role model such as Charlayne Hunter-Gault, but this letter written in 1979 by an eighty-year-old fan, which I spotted in her office, exemplifies it best:

> More power to you, dear Charlayne! Both evenings, which you conducted by yourself, were excellent. When you found you had no time for the usual spiel, you just warmly said "good night!" I got tears in my eyes for pride at how well you, a woman, handled yourself! In these two evenings, you have done so much for all of us women!
>
> *Lotte Fairbrook*

I SEE MY LIFE AS A CONTINUAL PROGRESSION, inasmuch as I've always done the same work—journalism—and that's what I see in the future. If there is any significant difference between my forties and fifties, it's that I've always shared my life, my professional development, and career with my kids. And now they are pretty much at an age where I don't have to devote quite as much psychic energy to them as I once did, although we are still very much a family and I am intimately involved with the decisions my daughter makes about her career and my son makes about college. It's a very liberating time because, while I had a career before my children were born and don't feel that they inhibited it, I did make certain career decisions because of them. I worked for almost ten years at *The New York Times,* mostly on the metropolitan staff, rather than going to the national or foreign staffs. That's why I came to "MacNeil-Lehrer"—I could do some of the more far-reaching news stories without having to leave New York. When they were little, I did not want to do the kind of traveling that being on the national or foreign staff would entail, which is often 50 to 75 percent of one's time. Now that my children are grown, I don't have the same demands on my personal life, and I've definitely increased my pace in terms of working.

I've always been a very confident person, and I just find myself growing more confident as I get older. This includes the confidence both to question and doubt myself without panicking about it. I feel that the more mature I become and the more experiences I have, the less insecure I feel about questioning. There's a time in your life when you feel you have to prove yourself in the world, and when you feel you have done that, it's a matter of fine-tuning.

I come from a family of people who are pretty hearty and live to be very old. They venerate age. My aunt Louise was old when she was young. Not that she was unattractive; she was very stylish, but she was mature and wise and settled. I never heard anybody in my family sit around and talk about getting old; and nobody ever made apologies or expressed any anxieties about being thirty or forty or fifty or sixty. Their lives just kept going on. So I have always loved birthdays.

Everywhere I go, when I mention that I'm fifty, people seem so surprised that I would say this above a whisper. Sometimes I see kids go into a catatonic state about being thirty or forty. The only time I can understand that is when somebody is in their late thirties or forties and hasn't had a child and wants to and is worried about the biological clock. Most of it is just routine anxiety about being older. It all has to do with how you feel about yourself—period.

Then you take everything else as it comes. If you feel positive about yourself, then the rest of it is somebody else's problem.

"MacNeil-Lehrer" is a totally nontraditional news program which changed the way news is reported on television. Because of that they have never demanded the traditional profile of so-called television anchors. I've never been asked or felt the pressure to say something different so that I would sound more like a television personality. Right after I joined the program, I thought I should take some voice coaching because I hadn't done any television work to speak of. I took a few voice lessons and thought, "This is not for me; this is not me. I don't want to sound like everybody else; I don't want to *be* like everybody else. I want to be *different*." Because I am different. I'm black. I'm a woman. I'm southern. And I happen to think that's how you get really good journalism, by having a variety of different personalities, backgrounds, colors, and creeds interact. I found affirmation in that at "MacNeil-Lehrer." For example, I change my hairstyle pretty frequently. They tease me about it, but they never once said, "Don't do that. You have to look the same all the time." If they did, I think I would have to leave television.

I think fantasy is absolutely essential to a happy life, and I feel very positive about it. In fact, I was just telling this young kid in prison to write a short story for me. He was interested in being a boxer at one point in his life. He said he didn't have a left jab, and I said, "So you could write a story and you could give yourself a left jab. You could start with the reality of your experience and then it can go anywhere, because that's what fiction is. You can make it come out the way you wanted it to." He's doing that. I think that's what fantasy is. This is a very intense life, and you have to find some release from it, or otherwise you'll go crazy. You might go crazy anyway. I never could have become a journalist if I hadn't had the capacity to fantasize, because in those days there weren't any black women—or men, for that matter—working in mainstream media, so-called "role models."

My role model, I guess, developed out of a fantasy life I had with my dolls and the comic strips. Brenda Starr was my fantasy role model. I loved this life of hers and thought it was very exciting. If I had not been given to fantasy, I never could have imagined myself doing something like that because there were roles set up for us, women like me, we knew "our place." That's where the title of my book comes from: *In My Place*. Our place was teaching or nursing—nothing wrong with that; it just wasn't what I wanted to do. Fantasizing enabled me to see beyond the limits of Jim Crow, and, while I didn't know how I was going to get there, I felt that I *could* get there and I fantasized about getting there and the way was made. I partly made it, but it got made.

I have very concrete models in my life of women who have aged beautifully, creatively, energetically, and productively. My grandmother was the first. She died in her eighties. She was active and productive until the last few years of her life. But even then her fantasies were what she lived openly, at least she articulated them. They were marvelous. She'd been married four times, and while she was very religious, she was no puritan. She had her little nip of Scotch. She didn't like Scotch-on-the-rocks because she thought the rocks adulterated the Scotch, so she would say, "I want it with no adulteration," meaning "neat." She's my sort of heroine. She was the one who introduced me to the world. In one sense she wasn't a worldly person; she went to third grade and then her mother took her out to work. But she read newspapers and taught herself to read. I wrote about her in *The New Yorker*.

My hope, not my fantasy, is to grow old in a positive way, not to become embittered about aging. On my fiftieth birthday, I'd had three ski lessons in my life and I went to the tallest mountain in Vail, Colorado, and skied down. It took me two and a half hours because after only three lessons, I still wasn't proficient. But I did it because I wanted to do something different. I wanted something that would say, "This is how I'm going to deal with aging." There were some *very old* women on the ski slopes having the best time.

I always want to be in love, too. I really like the state of being in love. With life, my husband, everything. My husband and I work at it; it gets a little tired sometimes, but we both recognize it, and we will do something to spark it back up.

For eight years of my life, I was an only child and tended to have an only child's frame of reference. I loved my time to myself. Now I take it, even if it's an hour or thirty minutes or even ten. I find I really have to fight for that space; I pursue it much more passionately than I've ever done. I have to have time to myself. My husband plays golf, and a lot of his buddies tease him because when he's out all day, he doesn't start to get fidgety about going home for dinner like the others. He laughs and tells them, "You don't know, my wife is so happy to have that house alone; I can stay out here till midnight and she wouldn't mind." I like having that time.

Concerning politics, I think everyone related the large number of women running for political offices to the Anita Hill/Clarence Thomas hearings, but I have seen this movement developing for a long time. I remember when Geraldine Ferraro was nominated for vice-president in 1986. I didn't see things shutting down after that. I saw many people discouraged, perhaps, but the seeds had been planted for this possibility. Shakespeare says there is a "tide in the affairs of men that when taken at the flood leads onto fortune." I think this is simply one of those tides. This tide has been flowing steadily and it is a ripeness, a fullness of time rather than something that springs fully armed from the head of Zeus. This didn't come from nowhere. Women were perched and ready and already moving. It's just that the media didn't pay that much attention. This has been one of the most stunningly open centuries for women in the history of the world. I've been talking about it for years now, the things that women are doing.

Women are going to be challenged to deliver. I think women *can* deliver. One of the changed dynamics we may begin to see is that rather than an isolated woman breaking through here or there, we will begin to get a critical mass in office. That's when women can be emboldened to really be powerful. I've seen situations in which women *do* get into positions of authority, but because they are surrounded by the same men who made the decisions all along, they are co-opted or in some way not permitted to or prevented from doing what they said would happen if they got into positions of power. Women have said they would bring a different sensitivity to issues, a different approach, a different style. So that remains to be seen; women will be challenged to do it differently. Is it really true that women are much more interested in mediation and conflict resolution, rather than war? Are they more inclined toward humanitarian responses to crisis? Or will they end up as Golda Meir, whom Ben Gurion described as "the best man" in his cabinet? It will be an interesting decade.

Political women need financial support; that's a critical ingredient for the success of women politicians. Maybe we can, in some way, change this crazy system of what it takes to run for public office. The amount of money it takes is obscene, but if that's the name of the game, then women have to get out and support women politicians on the basis of common interests and attitudes. Women have to be supported with cash resources, which is sort of the *sine qua non* of being successful in the political arena.

It is also important for women to communicate and share their personal experiences with each other. For example, the experience of menopause. Each of us has a different experience, but I know and have interviewed so many women who thought they were going crazy because there is so little information about it. Now the baby boomers are getting to be menopausal, and frank discussions are starting to emerge about hot flashes and vaginal dryness. I'm still searching for answers to the estrogen replacement therapy myself, and see how important it is to have discussions with other women.

I was talking to a friend of mine who is a year younger than me. I asked her why she didn't get braids like her sister's beautiful Ethiopian-style braids. She said, "I have night sweats and have to scratch my scalp, which I don't think I could do with those braids." I asked if she was taking estrogen and she said, "No, I think I can get through without it." I said, "You may be able to get through the night sweats and hot flashes, but you may encounter vaginal dryness because the vaginal walls begin to get thin and it makes intercourse painful. You can get topical estrogen for that." She looked at me; she was stunned. I found this out through my research, and through talking with women who are having trouble in their marriages because they couldn't figure out what was happening.

My own menopause has not been terribly disruptive—nothing ever drove me *too* nuts. I talked about it. I did research and stories about it. I informed myself. That's when I realized there is so little information available. We are such captives of whatever information is out there, which is mostly the product of male research. It's very important to have another woman friend, friends who are the same age or just a little older who can say, "No, you're not crazy. You may be depressed out of your mind, but it's a passing thing." Or, "This is how you can deal with that symptom." Let's face it, not all women in their fifties are healthy or positive. We can help each other by sharing our own positive ideas and attitudes.

I have never allowed myself to be defeated by sexism or racism or slowed down by them, even though I have experienced them both. I just step back and try to figure out how to plow through it, step over it or around it, so that my attitude about it is not one of anger or bitterness, because I keep going forward. I've always tried to affirm my difference and treated it as an opportunity and an added dimension to myself and my work. I've never tried to be something other than what I am.

When I interviewed Wangari Matthai, the Kenyan environmental activist, I asked her why women are so involved in the environmental movement, and she spoke about women projecting their own hopes for the future. In a sense, women are the natural nurturers; they nurture children. Wangari now sees them using their natural instinct to nurture the earth. So they are projecting their own nature onto this environmental movement, which in Wangari's case has become a political movement. She has inspired thousands of women in Africa to plant millions of trees. They receive fifty cents for every tree that survives for three months. But, in that context, the subsistence also gives them a feeling of empowerment. That's something one person can do. People like that have real moral authority because they don't fear dying; they have a commitment to something. That's what women have now that is refreshing and new. They have a real opportunity to assume their positions with moral authority because they're not tainted by the politics of the past. It remains to be seen, but the women we've seen taking their places in leadership positions today all over the world are not afraid. They may not want to be martyrs, but they are prepared to be if necessary; and that's what gives them their moral authority.

Women are uniquely positioned to bring something new and fresh to the world of "business as usual," "bankrupt politics," and I think that's their challenge. I just hope they will be true to themselves and to their nature. There's nothing wrong with being a nurturer and nurturing humanity. We can do that in the political arena, the halls of Congress, the White House, in hospitals where babies are suffering because they have no love and no parents. There are so many places where we could have an impact. Women begin with a clean slate. In a sense, we can do anything. We just have to appreciate that in ourselves and coalesce with others who feel that way; that could be men, too. In a world crying out for leadership, it seems women are properly positioned to step up to the line and play that role.

RUTH ZAPORAH

In my fifties, I feel ripely quiet. Life seems simpler; I am more appreciative. More of life seems funny to me, humorous and light. I consistently have a good time. It hasn't always been like that.

profile

"SHE JUST STOOD THERE IN A LITTLE BLACK DRESS and sang her heart out," Ruth Zaporah marveled. And as if the words alone might not convey the magnitude of what she was saying, she repeated: "Her *heart* out." Ruth was speaking of Edith Piaf, who she says—unequivocally and without hesitation—is the woman who has most influenced her life and work. Ruth had seen the "Little Sparrow" perform in the mid-1950s, in the famous Los Angeles nightclub the Mocambo. Although she was a dancer, not a singer, at age twenty-one it had been a formative experience. "I'd been trained as a traditional dancer, but that night I knew that my work would have to be about the heart being out. That's where my work comes from: Edith Piaf."

Ruth and I met in her home on a street up in the Berkeley hills that is nearly consumed by lush vegetation. (With its endless charm, nooks and crannies, romantic fireplaces, and breathtaking view, it's the kind of place that reminds you how stupid you were twenty years ago when you thought $30,000 was too high a price for a house like this. Now you couldn't touch it for under $500,000.) With her elfin face, hands, arms, and indeed her entire torso gesturing vividly, Ruth recounted to me the tale of her life and her work, which have been anything but traditional. "A dramatic transformation" is how she describes her life, a daily shift between being "a '50s upper-middle-class housewife" to being "an artist and beatnik." Today, she is the mother of three grown sons and a daughter. Then, like so many women of her generation, she struggled frantically to keep the components of children, work, art, and love in balance.

Ruth came to Berkeley in 1969 and formed, with two other dancers, the Berkeley Dance Theater and Gymnasium. But it is her Action Theatre that has given her a name, and which attracts students from around the country as well as from Europe. What is Action Theatre? Ruth describes it as a training process that allows people to express their moment-to-moment awareness, to be in the now, and to develop their physical, vocal, and verbal awareness skills. These awareness skills are important because, as Ruth suggests, "Most people don't know what their 'now' is, let alone how to express it." This sounded to me very Buddhist, like a training for mindfulness. "One hundred percent!" responded Ruth, "although I didn't know it originally. Now that's becoming evident." But she insists her training is not only a means of expressing the moment, it is also performance training. It is theater. "I'm also interested in the craft—the art of it, the form and clarity."

Ruth started dancing school at four years old, but her family says she was moving to music as an infant, dancing before she could walk. It's curious, then, that she does not now consider herself a dancer. She is also reluctant to categorize herself with performance artists—"They have a bad connotation in this country. Performance art usually means you don't have a lot of talent, just a big head"—and she describes herself as more of a "physical actor."

Not once during our conversation did Ruth use the term "creative"— a word, almost like "love," so overused it has lost its meaning and become a cliché. When I commented on this omission, she explained, "I think it's compartmentalizing: Now I'm creative, now I'm not. This is my creative work; this is my regular life. I think every moment is a creation."

I GOT MARRIED WHEN I WAS NINETEEN, and immediately had three children. I never thought about my life; it was carved out for me: to be a wife and a mother, to belong to a country club. I stayed in that marriage for twelve years, even though it was unhappy from the very get-go. Actually, we didn't even want to get married, but the presents had already been coming in so our families thought we were just being hysterical. They had to drug me to go down the aisle. I was so distraught, I knew it was the wrong thing. It took me twelve years to divorce the situation. I was the first person among my contemporaries to divorce. It was a dramatic transformation.

Through that marriage, my body was really a mess. I had migraine headaches, I had boils, I had eczema and my skin was always bandaged, I was smoking. I was depressed for many years. It got to the point where I couldn't breathe: it was either suicide or divorce. At the risk of shaming my family, which I did do, and losing all my friends, which I did do, and tearing my children apart—raising children then was not like it is today where every other child comes from a divorced family—I took an apartment with my children in Baltimore.

Being in the theater and in dance, I had already stepped out of my cultural milieu: that's what really supported the divorce, this other world. All through that twelve-year marriage I was dancing because I couldn't stand not to. So I had two lives: a traditional wife life, and the life of a beatnik with my artist friends—long hair, black clothes, cigarette smoking. I kept flipping back and forth every day between these two worlds, with lots of lies. And my body was falling apart.

After my separation, in 1968, a friend and I went to visit the Harvard summer biological center. There I met a man who lived in California. I immediately fell in love. I desperately wanted a reason to leave the East Coast—I was like the Scarlet Letter in my community—so a year later I took my kids and moved out to California to be with him.

Of course, then I realized I *had* to work. Up until that point, I had to work spiritually, but now I had to work because I had three kids to support. So I started teaching and performing. Teaching has always supported me. That first ten-year period in Berkeley was such fertile territory. Al Wunder, Terry Sendgraf, and I started the Berkeley Dance Theater and Gymnasium. From the beginning it was packed. We were interested in and taught improvisation, but from different angles. That was during the time when Gestalt theory was exploding, LSD was happening, people wanted to get in touch with their feelings and their bodies. There was so much support for our work.

Now it's a totally different scene; you're lucky if you can get a class together for young people. I don't have that problem because I've been teaching for so long, I have a name. People are buckling down. If they're doing any training, they want it to get them into a Broadway show or the American Conservatory Theatre. There's not the experimental fervor that went on in the '60s and '70s because we weren't worried about economics the way people are now. Then we were still very idealistic, interested in developing the self. So what better time to start teaching classes and exploring the self through the body. I was lucky.

My first marriage was very traditional; I was separating my husband's socks by color and following him around Europe on his trips, being *the* wife. And, obviously, suffering through it. Then my twenty-year relationship with my second husband was very volcanic. It has seen every arrangement possible: we've been married, we've been divorced, we've lived together, we've not lived together, we've lived together and seen other people, we've lived separately and seen other people *and* still seen each other. There was such passion and an incredible physical attraction.

I kept thinking, "If I just do the right thing it will work out. If I'm nice now, then later I'll be able to be myself." If Doris Day said all the right things to Rock Hudson, she'd get him in the end: that's the 1950s mentality. But you lose yourself in the process. So every wrenching away was, "I have to find myself." Then I'd find myself (or at least what I *thought* was myself), get strong, build up my resources, get my boundaries clear and think, "Okay, now I'm ready to handle it." Then the whole thing would happen again.

It seems like my biggest growing times have been when I've been single. In my work, my sense of self, my clarity: all the leaps and bounds have happened when I was single. When I'm in relationship, it takes up too much of my attention. I didn't grow up with any models for relationship, so I have to make it up, and that's what I'm struggling with. Some people grow up with a stronger sense of themselves than I did. I wasn't given that by my family—it was quite the opposite; but they were also coming from immigrant families, in the Jewish ghettos. My parents did what they could do. It strings through like a string of beads, and I'm the next bead. I really don't know how to be in relationship.

Just as the forms of the '50s at one point didn't work for me anymore, now the form of the present life I've constructed for myself is beginning to not work for me. I think a break with this life is going to happen during the next ten years. Where I live, the way I live—in this kind of house, in an urban environment, the kind of work I do—will be changing. I don't know what form it will take, but it will be much simpler, much emptier than this one.

What seems to be coming forward now is community, even more than relationship, "the man." Not that I'm uninterested in a relationship; I am. But lately, it's not something I've spent a lot of time yearning for, which I'm happy about, because I was in that place for a while. Up until a year and a half ago, when I was fifty-five, I have always been in relationship. This year and a half has been really new. I enjoy myself. I don't feel that there's a hole to be filled.

I think I will continue to work a lot during the next ten years. I want to be able to *stop* working, so I'm saving up. My brother and my father sat me down and told me it's time to start thinking about saving, so I've been thinking about that for the last six months. That's a new phase for me.

In my fifties I feel ripely quiet. Life seems much simpler; I am more appreciative. More of life seems funny to me, humorous and light. I consistently have a good time. It hasn't always been like that. I'm worming my way out of the darkness. I can say that now I feel pretty comfortable in just about every situation, whereas I used to be nonverbal, never able to express myself. I could never go to parties. I haven't done much therapy; I think it's been my work that's done the healing.

It's very hard for me to accept the slowing down and deterioration of my body. I'm a *body* person. I don't like aging. I watch my father, who is ninety. We are the same physical types. He still plays golf, but I see him struggle with the fact that he can't move the way he used to. I'm beginning to experience that. I work out *every* day. When I was thirty, I didn't work out at all. My body just took care of itself; now I have to put in time every day, and I'm obsessed with working out. If a day goes by, and I don't work out, I feel badly. I've been running since I was thirty-five. But that's beginning to take a toll on my joints, my knees, my feet, my hips. I can't run the way I used to, and probably shouldn't be running at all. My feet were X-rayed and the doctor said he would think that the feet in the X-ray belonged to an eighty-five-year-old; they are so abused and fractured and calcified. They're a mess. You can see I've been beating them up all my life.

I'm very strong. I'm not taking hormone replacement therapy, so I am countering with weight-bearing exercises—pushing, pulling, lifting, and pressing for my bones. And I'm eating right. I hope that will help to stave off the deteriorating aging phenomena that can happen to women. We probably weren't built to live past sixty-five; I think we are living longer than our bodies were built to live.

Menopause was relatively symptom-free for me. Occasionally, there were sweats, but they seemed to be more connected to moments of anxiety. Sweats were never bothersome to me because I've always sweated in my work. Some of my friends went through much more traumatic experiences than me. I read everything and I've asked my gynecologist if she thinks I should take anything. It's scary being postmenopausal today because you've got a horrible choice to make. I don't want to take hormone replacement. I've had two seriously dramatic experiences with the medical profession where they almost killed me.

One was twenty years ago, when I ruptured a disc in my back while dancing. I was in the hospital for three weeks in traction, and they were filling me with drugs because the pain was excruciating. Through this hazy space, I saw three doctors come in to my room, stand at the foot of my bed, and say if they didn't get a neurological reading in the next forty-eight hours, they were going to take a piece of bone from my hip and fuse it to my neck. That would have been the end of my dance career. I was determined they weren't going to do that. Immediately, I stopped taking the medication and started focusing. Within two days they got a positive neurological reading. I dealt with it instead of just lying there, hoping they were going to fix me. I left the hospital and got away from that whole system.

Then one night, about four years ago, my heart started fibrillating and continued for hour after hour. It was terrifying—it would pound loudly and then stop altogether. Finally, I called the doctor and he said to go to the Emergency Room immediately. I stayed in the hospital that night. They put me on digitalis and took more and more tests. One cardiologist wanted to put me on beta-blockers for the rest of my life. This went on for six months while I'm going from cardiologist to cardiologist, knowing the whole time I'm perfectly healthy.

I got really desperate. I was down in Venezuela with my three sons and we were going into the Amazonian jungle. Emotionally, I was out of control with these drugs. I've always been a very stable person, not overly emotional. But the heart drugs were making me nuts. I came back from the Amazon thinking this was intolerable. So I called a friend who is an "imaginative" doctor, and he helped me get off the medicine and I've been fine ever since. The gift of that whole experience was that I realized I was eventually going to die.

Death has always been a major influence in my work as well as life, improvisation, being in the present, because that's what's always happening. Somebody's always dying. Every moment. Even as you and I talk. I mainly do trainings that have beginnings and endings. Twice a year I do a month-long training, and people come from all over the United States and Europe. We meet four hours every day and we die. We do. We die together. They are definitely in their death throes. They know the old forms are not working for them—the old ways of being unconscious, of being on automatic.

One woman came up to me after class today and she said, "I notice when I talk to people, I laugh a lot; they'll say something and I'll laugh; this kind of noise comes out of me. I'm not really laughing, but it's a laugh-like noise." Her noticing that is a kind of death. That laughing is going to die, and when it dies there will be a new space. By noticing it, she's going to let it go. It is a transformation. It's fun, and it hurts. It's life. It's everything.

This work is healing. It's good medicine. I see people more alive, day by day. But that's not why I do it; I don't work "in order to do" anything to the other. There's not a lot of money in this work. I do it because it feels great and I have a good time. It's my practice place. The place that I go where I'm complete and full.

I've raised four kids. That's a lot, especially because I was one of the kids; we grew up together. We experimented with all the same things at the same time: sex and drugs. It was both good and bad—for all of us. I've never been the usual PTA kind of mother. I always worked and my kids always came along on my work. All my kids know how to stage manage and how to do lights. They know how to do bulk mailings. They've been very much involved with my kooky friends. I've had to juggle being with them and being in my theater life, so I feel that necessity forced me to compromise greatly in each. There were definitely some areas of parenting I neglected because of my performance work and teaching. And there were areas of my performance work I neglected because I was parenting. It's all worked out okay, my four children are now fairly healthy, kindly people with good values; they all feel strongly for the planet and the people of the planet, and my work is in a good place. But there were many times when I thought it wasn't going to work out at all.

I belong to a group called the Dharma Witches. We've been meeting once a month for seven years. Everyone in the group is involved with Buddhism in some way. We wanted to figure out what would be a woman's spiritual practice. One of the major questions we asked is, What are we, as women in our middle years, doing here on this planet? What is our role and responsibility? For myself, I wonder when I will be too old to perform. That's a consideration, because I sometimes feel funny getting up in front of my audiences, which are mainly young people. Who wants to see an older woman up there improvising? It's an issue of vanity: I don't look as good as I used to. My body isn't as tight as it used to be. When do I stop coloring my hair and let it go gray? When can I be a gray-haired performer? I used to imagine myself having long gray braids when I was old. I said to someone the other day, "This is the last time I'm coloring my hair. I'm on my way to my gray braids now." But I've said that before. Then the gray starts coming out . . .

There is a place for traditional, older actresses. But I do another art form, although I notice it's changing. I'm moving less than I used to and speaking more than I did before. The content has teachings in it, even though that's not what I think about when I do it. So I'm finding my role as a middle-aged performer and teacher. I'm finding that my performing is teaching and my teaching is performing.

GLORIA ALLRED

I like *being in my fifties. I don't think it's anything we should be ashamed of. We should get medals for having survived considering what women have to go through to reach the age of fifty and the obstacles they face. It's a real test of survival—what women endure everyday.*

profile

Cautious, careful people, always casting about to preserve their reputation and social standing, never can bring about a reform. Those who really are in earnest must be willing to be anything or nothing in the world's estimation, and publicly and privately in season and out, avow their sympathies with despised and persecuted ideas and their advocates, and bear the consequences.

SUSAN B. ANTHONY

"WE HAVE TO KEEP FIGHTING; WE JUST HAVE TO KEEP FIGHTING," the woman blurted out as she grabbed at my arm. She was in tears, but had the glint of a promising prizefighter in her eye. "She's wonderful, isn't she—Gloria!" The woman was a potential client of the feminist activist attorney Gloria Allred, and we had this encounter as I was going into Gloria's office and she was coming out. I could only guess what her situation might be, but I recognized the intensity of her anxiety as periodically my own: a result of the fear that many women experience—the fear of losing what we have and the fear of not getting what we need. Unself-consciously, she echoed the words of countless suffragists and feminists who have fought in the past and continue today to fight for the rights of women.

Gloria Allred represents many such women through her firm Allred, Maroko, Goldberg, and Ribakoff, which is located on Miracle Mile of Wilshire Boulevard only two blocks from the Los Angeles County Museum. Her elegant office is appointed with English antiques and feminist memorabilia. From the fourteenth floor, the office has a sweeping view of West Hollywood and the Hollywood hills, including the famous HOLLYWOOD sign. We met in the spring of 1992, only one week after the looting and rioting that followed the verdict acquitting four Los Angeles police of brutally beating Rodney King. An appliance store opposite her building had been looted, and the view from her office was of dense smoke from arson. Gloria was devastated by the outbreak of violence, and saw it as a significant setback for civil rights, for which she has fought for more than thirty years.

Designated by *Los Angeles* magazine as one of the "thirty most powerful people in Los Angeles," she has also been referred to by the magazine as one of the "seventy-eight most interesting people in L.A." I noticed a pair of red boxing gloves in the corner of her office. She explained that she had received them in the mail from a woman who said in the accompanying note, "I think of you as a fighter; you should have these." Apparently, that woman wasn't alone in her view of Gloria: *US* magazine has named her "the Feistiest Feminist Lawyer in the West." Although she has gained the reputation for being controversial, abrasive, strident, and shrill, I found her to be unfailingly gracious, while remaining an outspoken and relentless advocate for women's rights.

Gloria is the Friday evening commentator on KABC TV's "Eyewitness News," and she sees her television and radio work as an opportunity to educate women. "Most people don't learn about women's rights in school," she explains. "We must use the mass media to educate them about their lives." She discusses a variety of disparate issues, both legal and political, ranging from Madonna to rape, from AIDS and abortion to Nelson Mandela. On the day of our interview, Gloria was buoyed by the fact that she had been nominated for an Emmy Award for a debate she had done on the Anita Hill-Clarence Thomas hearings.

Gloria had also just received word that her thirty-year-old daughter, Lisa, who had previously practiced law in New York, had passed the California Bar examination. Ecstatic, she made me promise not to reveal the news until she made the announcement that her daughter would now join her firm. Lisa is a frequent reference point in her mother's conversation. Gloria glistened when she affirmed, "I'm happy to say my daughter is a strong feminist." Feminism is a unifying factor in her family: Gloria's granddaughter, Sarah, was born on Women's Equality Day, 1989.

A woman of both style and substance, her jet-black hair is a dramatic backdrop for brilliant red lipstick and a vermilion-colored suit, which together make a visual statement of her name. Gloria earned a master's degree in English education at New York University, taught at an all-black boys' school in Philadelphia (where she was raised), then moved to Los Angeles to teach in the Watts ghetto after the 1965 riots. Appalled by the plight of female teachers, and becoming aware of the growing feminist movement, Gloria began asking about the rights that women *didn't* have. This led her to attend Loyola University Law School, and to her subsequent practice of seventeen years. She believes that being a feminist should be a requirement for all attorneys and all judges because, as she explained in her usual forthright manner, "If you're not a feminist, you're a bigot—and a bigot doesn't belong in the courtroom or on the bench."

Asked why there is an early-twentieth-century English bobby's uniform on display in her office, she replied, "I bought it, complete with handcuffs, to remind people that thousands of women were arrested by police officers in uniforms like that just for trying to win the fundamental right for women to vote. It's only because of the courageous efforts of the suffragists that we eventually won the vote. We forget that women fasted in protest while they were in prison—many of them were forcibly fed—and many died working for women's rights. Having this uniform in my office gives me the opportunity to tell people a bit of women's her-story that they should know." With Gloria Allred as our champion and counsel, women are still walking shoulder-to-shoulder in the spirit of Victorian suffragists.

I'M TRYING TO REMEMBER IF THERE WAS EVER A TIME when I *wasn't* a feminist. A feminist is a person who believes in legal, social, political, and economic equality for women with men. I think the reason most of us are feminists—and I would include myself—is because of some of the life experiences we've had. We have not been treated equally or fairly, and that's why we feel so deeply that feminism is important.

There were a number of experiences that were an important part of the "making of a feminist." My first job after I graduated from college was at a department store. I earned less than a man who had the position of assistant buyer because, I was told, I probably didn't have a family to support and that he, being a man, probably would have to support a family. In fact, that particular man was a bachelor and I was a single parent raising a child by myself. I saw this as an inequity based solely upon my gender.

Another experience had to do with my having an abortion after I was raped at a time when abortion was illegal for doctors to provide. I almost died from it. This was a case of the government deciding that it wants to control women. Such decisions have resulted in the death of many women, the maiming of many women, the suffering of many women.

In the case of rape, the violence against women is, in large part, due to the concept of many men that women are there to be subordinated, controlled, and terrorized. That's the opposite of feminist thinking. So having been raped myself made me feel more strongly about the right of women to be free from such violence and suffering and to be treated equally and brought into the mainstream of American life. Then, of course, I have a daughter who is thirty, and I also have a granddaughter. I certainly want a better world for them.

I raised my daughter as a single mother for about five years or so, and then I remarried. It was a long marriage—nineteen years. Now I'm divorced and have been a single woman again since 1986. I have to say that at first I dreaded being single because I'm used to being married, used to having someone around every day. But I knew it was important to be able to go about my life alone, and I have to say it's been a wonderful experience. I like the independence, I like the freedom. I'm not saying I would never marry again, but I'm very happy the way I am now. It's just a wonderful freedom that, frankly, I really never knew before. I consider myself reasonably liberated, although I have a lot to learn still, as we all do, about what that can truly mean. I have wonderful friends, a wonderful family, a very exciting professional life. Not only am I busy, but I have a lot of fulfillment. There are relationships other than a marriage that are also important and very fulfilling in our lives.

When I was much younger, of course, I thought of fifty as being very old. I had many stereotypes of what it is like to be in your fifties. Now that I am fifty, I have to say I feel as though I'm much younger. I look at my granddaughter and my grandson and I say, "I can't believe they're really my grandchildren." It's wonderful. But I don't think of myself as the kind of person who is the fifty that I once thought fifty was. I wouldn't want to go back to the time when I was nineteen. Some people wish for the time when they were younger; I *like* being in my fifties. I shock a lot of men by telling them how old I am. I think they're shocked for a couple of reasons: one is that they're not used to women telling their age, especially if they are in their fifties and single and dating. I even shock some women friends of mine, too. Sometimes they ask, "Why do you have to say that?" And I reply, "I don't think it's anything we should be ashamed of. We should get medals for having survived, considering what women have to go through to reach the age of fifty and the obstacles we face." It's just incredible, a real test of survival, what women endure every day.

Now that I'm in my fifties I feel I'm better able to cope than when I was nineteen. I understand more about life. I'm in my reality phase and have been for some time. I understand the difference between a romantic view of the world and a view of reality, and I think I am based in reality—which doesn't mean I don't enjoy fantasies or romance, but I feel that most of my decisions (if not all) are based in reality. I still have ideals, but I also look at what can be accomplished given the reality. I also look at the realities to meet the ideals. Feminism has been an enormous help to me in making sense out of life and in coping with reality for myself and for my clients.

I have never had plastic surgery, and, of course, we now know the destruction and devastation and suffering that so many women have been subjected to because of the silicone breast implants. I've done a television commentary on that. I just would ask women to move with a great deal of caution before they choose to have that type of plastic surgery, to be sure they know what all the risks and consequences are as well as the benefits. I wouldn't do it. Although I'm now at an age where I feel that I would never want to rule anything out. But I will say this: I cannot imagine a set of circumstances which would ever lead me to have plastic surgery for elective reasons. The benefits do not outweigh the risks.

Often a woman's concern about aging has to do with getting a man or keeping a man, or sometimes it's getting or keeping another woman. And the feeling that aging is going to impede them in the accomplishment of that goal. Some of them deny that and say, "I'm just getting plastic surgery for myself." But I think they're afraid that if they look older, they will not look as attractive and therefore either lose their partner or not find one. It's definitely a sexist attitude that we have in our society. Many more women are worried about these issues than are men. A young, sexy woman without any wrinkles is certainly set up as an ideal by the image makers on television and in commercial filmmaking. It's difficult to say that an individual woman should fight against the image makers. I'm not in the business of telling women what they should do in that regard. I, myself, will not buy into that, so if and when I develop more wrinkles than I have now, I'll wear them as medals of survival and not be concerned about them.

I survived menopause. I don't remember having mood swings—for many women, that's a stereotype. It is shocking to me, though, to learn that the medications that are currently being prescribed for postmenopausal women (estrogen and progesterone) are *not* well-studied before they are prescribed. The medical literature does not know to a certainty, or even to a near-certainty, what the risks of those hormones are. That is, they think it might cause a decrease in heart disease, but it *might* cause an increase in breast cancer—they're not sure. Yet millions of women are being given prescriptions for those medications and they are taking them. To me, it's another example of women as guinea pigs. The government hasn't made it a priority to properly fund the research for this important issue.

I am fortunate that I have excellent health and am able, I hope, to help other women and inspire them to find their own strength and their own courage, and to continue to meet life's challenges in a successful way, because that's what we need to do. I can't do it *for* them. I can do it *with* them. They need to find their own courage and then inspire others. It's like the suffragists said, "Each one tell ten to tell ten to tell ten." So what we need to do is be supportive of each other and work together. Not just in law but in *every* aspect of life. I'm fortunate to have wonderful women friends. In fact, sometimes we wonder among ourselves why men can't be more like our women friends, because we are so supportive of each other.

Supposedly, 1992 is the "Year of the Woman." My hope is that every day is the Day of the Woman. We have to work to ensure that it happens. There is certainly an increase in the number of women running for elective office, and that's important, because women need to be involved in public policy—we *can* make a difference. I've supported many women who are running. I don't think we could do a *worse* job than the men have done. It's important for women to win offices throughout this nation—not only on a local level, but also at the state and national level. Of course, I would love to live to see the day when we have a woman in the White House. And I don't mean as First Lady, I mean as President of the United States. I subscribe to the slogan of the National Women's Political Caucus that "a woman's place is in the house—the House of Representatives."

Many people have asked me if I will run for an office. I'm not interested at this time. I really like what I'm doing, I'm challenged by work, and I feel there are very few private law firms working with a focus to assert women's rights. I'm fortunate to be doing the work I'm doing. So I have no plans to run for office in the near future, but I won't rule anything out for the far future—which would be, by my definition, after the next five years.

Part of the issue, too, is that if I did run for office, I might have to water down my views or worry about losing votes if I say this or that. I don't want to be worrying about that or looking over my shoulder. I just want to say what I think we need. I want to point at the wrongdoers and say, "You're perpetrating a wrong against women." I feel that, to some degree, I would be hampered if I were to run for office. I see my position inside *and* outside the system as being a strong advocate for women.

In a way, I don't think that any of us can be successful unless we're all successful. And since we're not all successful, I can't think that I am in any way that is really meaningful. I can talk about conventional success, obviously, as my law firm is considered a successful law firm. We are doing work that is important in the community, important to individuals, and we are prospering. I think we have a long way to go in women's rights, in changing and enforcing laws, and in protecting women. I won't think women are successful politically until at least half of all the elected offices are held by women; until half the legal profession is populated by women lawyers; until half of *every* occupation is populated by women—women at all levels, not just at the bottom level; until women are assuming their fair share of responsibility at home but not more. We have a long way to go.

It's important for everyone to have meaningful work. But work has often been too narrowly defined. Some people define it as only when they work outside the home, but work inside the home is also very meaningful. The job of nurturing and supporting children is also important, but women need to have their options. They need to be able to exercise them. So we need to be sure that women get the education they deserve and have a right to, and we also need to open up all levels of job opportunities so that women can aspire to and achieve many, many types of occupational goals they haven't yet achieved or have achieved only in token numbers because there is still so much sex discrimination—it is continuous and pervasive and systematic.

We need more role models. My first role model when I was growing up was my great aunt, who was the first woman heart surgeon at Children's Heart Hospital in Philadelphia. She always amazed me, because as long as I knew her, I never saw her cook a meal. She was the only woman I knew as I was growing up who didn't cook, and yet she managed to survive. I never knew when I was little how she got her food. And she never married nor had any children; that was very unusual in those days. She was a role model because she was very bright, well-educated. She didn't seem to care what the world thought, but she made an important contribution to the community. She believed in me and wanted me to succeed. I never really knew why, but I was happy that she did. My parents had an eighth-grade education, and even though they believed in me, it was important to have this aunt, Dr. Rachel Ashe, also take an interest in me.

As far as aging goes, my hope is that I *will* age, considering what the alternative is. I think emotionally I have the strength to deal with whatever life has in store. I've dealt with some extraordinarily difficult crisis situations. Most of what I deal with is crisis in human lives every day. I've dealt with it for my clients and I've dealt with it within my own family, with my dad, who just died recently. He and I waged a battle for over a year for his life. We won many battles together before the final one occurred. So I think I have a very realistic view of what life can have in store.

My father was in and out of the hospital on life-support systems, and I was told early on that he was going to die. He was eighty-nine years old, and why not just let him go. He had all kinds of tubes and life support. I was told he wasn't going to live through the night, and then through the weekend. I had to inform the doctors that my father did not want to die, I didn't want him to die, and the rest of the family didn't want him to die. We were going to fight for his life and we expected them to do the same. As someone I know said, "Tell them getting old is not a capital crime for which you should have to give your life."

We fought, and against all odds—the doctors called it a "miracle"—we got him out of the hospital and set up a hospital at home. He had a life for over a year longer. He was, of course, far more courageous than I was. I think I have an idea about the beginning of life and the end of life because I've seen both in the last few years. I've seen my grandchildren born and my dad die.

We have to do so much more in the area of care for the elderly. That's a whole other area. In a way I wish I had more than one life or that I could live a thousand lives at one time within this life. There are so many other important issues I'd like to get involved with. The elderly need much more in the way of rights and opportunities.

In terms of spirituality, I would say I have a strong spiritual side. Although I'm Jewish, I don't belong to any temple. But I have the values of the Jewish community, which is a sense of duty to the family and the community. We learn this from the time we are very young as Jewish people. It really is a duty, not just something you choose to exercise or choose not to exercise.

I don't know what my concept of God is, but there definitely is a force or forces that can't be explained. I'm thankful I'm here. I'm trying to lead a moral life. I try to be a person of conscience. That's going to be different for different people. I try to practice what I believe in and live my beliefs in my personal life as well as my political life. If I'm on a date, the guy can't believe I pay half the check. I don't do this just when the lights go out. I *live* my values as much as humanly possible, whether other people are looking or not because I have to be accountable to myself.

As I get older, I'd like to learn more about the spiritual side, because it's fascinating to me. There are many religions that have something to offer us to learn from. They all have some common truths or beliefs that are valuable in terms of guidance for living. But I will say that feminism has been a core, a rock, and a guiding principle for me.

I'm happy to be alive; very thankful to have lived to this age. I really think of every day as an absolute gift. There is a reason why I have this gift. I don't know if I'll ever know what it is, but I know I should live my life in a way that I am responding to the gift, in a way that is appropriate, making sure that my life is meaningful to other people as well as to myself. It's exciting to me. I see women coming into my law firm, crying, absolutely broken up, and I work with them over the years; I see them grow and become stronger and appreciate their own strength. Now they would not recognize the people they were when they first came in. Sometimes even their voices change—from a child's high voice to an adult's lower voice; they go from being completely hunched over to standing up straight, being proud of themselves. They begin organizing groups to help others. They may picket, testify in the legislature, run for public office, write books, whatever; they become women they can be proud of and women who are inspiring to others.

As women we must keep up our courage. Even though Susan B. Anthony had been struggling to win the right to vote and it wasn't achieved in her lifetime, her final words on her deathbed were, "Failure is impossible." It takes a great deal of courage for women to survive what they have to endure, because they are second-class citizens, subordinated, taken advantage of, betrayed, exploited and abused, cheated out of that which is theirs, treated with little dignity and respect. Women must have courage. That's what is needed. They should stand up, speak out, and fight back.

MARY ELLEN MARK

Creatively, I feel that I'm in my prime right now. I feel totally prepared to do my strongest work yet.

profile

Whenever the intensity of looking reaches a certain degree, one becomes aware of an equally intense energy coming towards one through the appearance of whatever it is one is scrutinizing.

JOHN BERGER, *Keeping a Rendezvous*

THE FACES ARE HAUNTING: A HETEROGENEOUS COMPILATION: "Tiny," a runaway street kid in Seattle; the sick and the dying at Mother Teresa's Missions of Charity in Calcutta; a hydrocephalic girl in a hospital in Turin, Italy; radiant children at Perkins School for the Blind in Massachusetts; the Damm family sitting in their battered car in Los Angeles—one example of America's incalculable homeless; glue addicts in Khartoum, Sudan; members of a gypsy camp in Barcelona, Spain; a young teenager about to give birth in New York; Ku Klux Klansmen at an Aryan Nations Congress in Idaho; autistic children in Connecticut; Marlon Brando, bald, with a thumb-sized beetle on his head, during the filming of *Apocalypse Now;* a traveling circus performer in India whose head seems surrealistically suspended by his elephant's trunk.

The photographs of Mary Ellen Mark are metaphors. She explains, "What you look for in a picture is a metaphor, something that means something more, that makes you think about things you've seen or thought about. What you look for is a symbol of something in everyone's life. Suffering is the great universal equalizer."

When I interviewed her in the winter of 1992, she was enjoying "a mid-life retrospective" of her work. A book and traveling exhibit were both titled, *Mary Ellen Mark: 25 Years.* Along with Sebastiao Salgado and Susan Meiselas, Mary Ellen is one of the most important documentary photographers working today. There is a seamless quality to her twenty-five years of photography, and her work displays an enigmatic power and social consciousness in the tradition of Dorothea Lange, Margaret Bourke-White, Henri Cartier-Bresson, and W. Eugene Smith.

Besides an obvious catholic curiosity, Mary Ellen's photographs display a bias of the imagination through which a highly developed emotional intelligence informs her work. She makes careful and respectful images of individuals. Hers is not a formulaic photography—there is nothing artificial or predigested about it—she is not an illustrator of the homogenized. This distinction is important in a world of instantaneously recognized pop images, a world in which many photographers have become as well-known as the famous faces they photograph. Such is not the case with Mary Ellen, who relies on a certain anonymity in order to photograph a diversity of unusual situations and people whom she calls the "unfamous."

Mary Ellen befriends her subjects (and often their animals) and lives their lives—on their terms, on their turf—for as long as she can. For thirty-six days, for example, she lived locked in the security ward of Oregon State Hospital. She admits, "The longer I stay, the closer I get to my subject." Mary Ellen shows an obvious willingness to improvise, and her means of making contact with others is uncontrived: she is present and honest with her subjects, and her responses to them are spontaneous. There is nothing false about her appreciation of them, and she is the first to acknowledge that it is through the gifts from the people she photographs that she has become what she is today.

During our time together, I felt Mary Ellen's intense and focused presence. At our prearranged meeting place—one of the elegant small hotels in San Francisco, the Stanford Court (where she had been staying in order to attend the opening of her exhibition at the Robert Koch Gallery)—she rushed into the lobby, ten minutes late, dressed with the presumed flair of an artist who loves silver jewelry and who makes her life and living traveling across continents. Her henna-red hair, worn in a single thick braid, swung down her back like a pendulum—a steady reminder of the enormous tasks to be done in a limited amount of time. Her vulnerability is visible beneath her own "streetwise" persona; her manner, unpretentious.

Her home base is New York City, where she lives with her husband, filmmaker Martin Bell; her studio, Falkland Road, is on Spring Street in SoHo. Mary Ellen revealed that the stability of her marriage has anchored her life. Born and raised in Philadelphia, Mary Ellen's childhood was difficult. Both her mother and father endured symptoms of manic depression. Her father was in and out of institutions, and his homecoming often erupted in displays of physical violence between her parents. Perhaps her own upbringing has helped her to intuitively understand and champion the underdog.

It was in graduate school at the Annenberg School for Communication at the University of Pennsylvania where she picked up her first camera (a Leica, a brand she has continued to use along with Nikon, Hasselblad, and Rolieflex) and her life's devotion was set into action. Mary Ellen recalls, "From the very first night, I became obsessed by photography. I knew I had a chance of being good."

For the thirty years during which photography has held her passion, Mary Ellen Mark has proven herself to be intuitive, disciplined, compassionate, diplomatic, single-minded, and a "gypsy." Her work has been contained in six books and published in countless periodicals, such as *LIFE, The New York Times Magazine, National Geographic, Rolling Stone, Time, Vanity Fair, Esquire,* and *Art in America.*

Mary Ellen's work has the content of an engagement with larger social issues. Her portraits present us with a physical reality, but it is the metaphorical reality that holds our stare and prompts us to know more about the subjects—those conventionally thought of as saints or sinners—who inhabit an atypical or marginal segment of society.

Her photographs could be seen as a litany of melancholy portraits that go directly to the viewer's emotional center, into the dark rooms of the soul. We think, "There but for the grace of God go I," when we see her study of heroin addicts or the homeless or the blind. The existence of fate or destiny in each of our lives is revealed to us in Mary Ellen's photographic oeuvre—a library of photographs documenting the human condition. We see the raw exposure of human beings devoid of the persona behind which most of us live our lives. The *New York Times* described her work as "an essentially tragic and apolitical vision of life which doesn't distinguish between the suffering that is inherent in life and that caused by social forces."

Thirteenth-century mystic Meister Eckardt referred to an intangible reciprocity when he wrote, "The eye with which I see God is the same eye with which he sees me." Mary Ellen Mark's images have a reciprocity of looking at and being seen. There is a parity, a symmetry—a matching and meeting of energies.

While viewing her photographs, I am aware of a light that streams through many of them. The light itself becomes a subject interacting with or supporting the figures, and seems to suggest that even in the midst of illness and destitution and hopelessness there is another source that can sustain us. This is especially true when Mary Ellen documents those imprisoned by social institutions, or those limited by their own blindness—physical or figurative.

Mary Ellen Mark doesn't think of her work as necessarily spiritual. "If what you mean by spiritual is an underlying connection between all things and a desire to create images that are larger than life, then yes, my work is spiritual; but if what you mean is religious, then no, my work is not spiritual." When I think of her life and her work, which have become meshed like the net of a fisherman, I am reminded of the final verse of an Eskimo Inuit song:

> And yet, there is only
> One great thing,
> The only thing:
> To live to see in huts and on journeys
> The great day that dawns,
> And the light that fills the world.

WHEN I FIRST STARTED IN THE '60s, there were fewer women photographers. Although there had been a great tradition of female photographers like Dorothea Lange, Margaret Bourke-White, and Julia Margaret Cameron—it was still somewhat of an oddity. But I never felt that being a woman photographer in a traditionally men's field was a hindrance. I've never used feminine powers to manipulate, and I hate women who do.

I just approached photography as a *person*. There is one advantage to being a woman in documentary work, and that is: people in general are less threatened by women. If I'm wandering around in a tough neighborhood and I meet a woman, or come to her house and knock on the door, it's easier for me to get into her house. If I were a man, her husband might think I was making a pass at his wife, or she might be afraid of me. So, in that sense, being a woman has been an advantage. As far as working in a predominantly male profession: I've always just put on blinders and gone ahead. That's all you can do. Given that, I absolutely know it is much tougher being a woman—all the way around—in all professions.

Today I went to the hair salon across the street to have my hair shampooed. On my way out I noticed a woman sitting there who was a lot older than me—well into her seventies—she just looked great. She was full of the silver jewelry I love, and I thought, "If I could look like her when I'm that age it would be great." She was totally natural.

The whole idea of being an aging woman in our society is tough. Women can't have children past a certain age—they're considered old—whereas a man has almost eternal youth. That in itself is a big, big difference. I made a deliberate decision not to have children. I never entertained the thought that I could have kids doing the kind of work I do. I always realized what a huge commitment having a child is. I'm not saying you can't have children if you're a photographer—many women have done it. But they do a different kind of photography—usually their work is done more in one place or in a studio. But with my work, I travel constantly and Martin does too. There's no stability for a child.

I have many friends, some much younger than me, who have children now. I see them with their adorable kids and I'm happy for them, but I don't feel any pangs of envy. I'm happy for them and recognize that kind of commitment is immense. Perhaps if I'd had children in my twenties, I would be glad now; but again, I don't know how I could have done that because I was wandering around the world even then.

What gives my life meaning? Certainly, my relationship with Martin. I feel so fortunate to have met someone I deeply care about, someone I respect. And who respects me also and cares about me. And, of course, my work. What else is there? Love and work. I've grown enormously in the past ten years as a photographer, and a lot of that growth has to do with Martin's help. He not only taught me a great deal technically, but provided that sense of calmness that comes with a solid relationship. We both feel we can focus more on our work.

While Martin is completely involved in his own work, he's very supportive of my work as well. He always has been. We've been together since 1980. That's a long time. I got married when I was forty; I never thought I would marry again. I was briefly married in college—it was not an unhappy marriage, but I thought we were much too young and I wanted some years of freedom. When I met Martin, things just fell into place—he's great to be with. He's like a great friend. I love him; I do. He's a strong and wonderful person. I respect him. We're both very involved in our work. I think that's important.

The fact that I met someone was really surprising to me because it happened when I least expected it. I wanted a relationship, but I'd given up. When I met Martin, our relationship was so easy and nice from the very first moment. There was never the kind of stress that can happen early on in relationships where no one wants to make a commitment. There was no stress. I hate stress on any level.

Martin just made a new film—a narrative, not a documentary—called *American Heart*. It's a story about a man who gets out of prison (played by Jeff Bridges) who tries to put his life back together with his teenage son. It's about being born in the wrong bed and how difficult it is to reshape our destiny. Martin is now working on a film project with John Irving, which will take place in India. It's called *Son of the Circus*. It's a wonderful script, and hopefully we'll be able to put that film together. I think *American Heart* will establish Martin as a fine director, and that can only help get this next film going.

Probably the most important thing photography has taught me is to recognize the common threads in humanity. For instance, whatever bed you're born into generally shapes your destiny. It is very difficult to change that. Someone from a poor welfare family, no matter how bright or precocious a child they may be, has fewer chances of having a blessed life than someone who is born into a privileged environment. Certainly, this sense of destiny is exaggerated more so in countries in the Third World, where people are more culturally and socially locked into a pattern. Here in the United States, there is a bit more chance to overcome the social standing you are born into, but not much.

As a young teenager, I did everything I could to be as normal as possible because I wanted to be popular. I became a cheerleader, every American high school girl's dream—at least it was in the '50s. I wanted to be accepted. I still had that need to please and be accepted through the first years of college. But when I started to photograph, I changed. I became less concerned about what people around me thought about me.

As a child I had an unhappy home life. My parents were emotionally unbalanced. It's sad but true. My father was in and out of mental hospitals—he had several nervous breakdowns from the time I was very young. My mother was also an emotionally unstable woman. So I witnessed real violence—physical and psychological—in my home between them. I witnessed my father being carried off several times to mental hospitals. And one day, when I was a teenager, he had a severe heart attack and I saw him die right in front of me. But, in a positive sense, my childhood gave me this drive to be free and to succeed on my own without the support some people have from their parents.

The creative drive or the need to produce great work is all-encompassing, and sometimes it drives you mad because it never gives you a chance to rest. There is no relief or release. There is a gnawing feeling in the pit of my stomach that sometimes I hate. I look at other people who don't have this desire, and often their lives are much happier and more peaceful. Creatively, I feel that I'm in my prime. I feel totally prepared to do my strongest work yet. I feel full of energy, and physically I'm as strong as I've ever been. I feel very fit.

There have been so many extraordinary experiences around my work. Like the time I worked with the prostitutes in India, or the six weeks I lived in a mental hospital—I made friends with amazing women who were so open and raw. Just the day-to-day living becomes a great adventure when you're involved in a project that you really care about. There are many more great memories—like the circus in India, working with the street kids in Seattle, photographing Mother Teresa's missions. It's hard to single one out, because they all have something so special. I guess it would be like asking someone with many children which child they preferred.

Photography gives a certain immortality to those photographed. I've always felt I'd rather give that immortality to people who wouldn't necessarily ever have it. When I worked on movie sets in the '60s and '70s, a photographer could have total access—real human contact with actors and directors—and make real photographs. It's very different now, in the sense that most actors only feel comfortable in showing a very safe and stylized version of themselves. Because of that the photographs of famous people today are much more contrived. It is not very often you see pictures of actors that touch their souls, and those are the kind of pictures I would wish to take. But it is very difficult—even with great access to a famous person. In the many years that I have photographed, I've gotten only a few images of the famous that I think transcend the fact that this is a very recognized face.

As a photographer you're always taking something. You have to come to terms with that fact. But basically, that's what can make an image great—someone has allowed you to see something private, they have given you a part of themselves. Many people say to me, "Most of your work is about marginal people." But that's not only what my work is about. I'm interested in what motivates people's minds and lives. I'm interested in those things that cross human and cultural boundaries—this common bond that we all share. If I pick people who are less advantaged, it's because I really want to say we're all the same. I'm touched by these people. I choose to photograph people I care about, people I feel are worth getting close to.

For years magazines were my grants, they funded my personal work—and I always looked at them that way. At this point it is much more difficult to find magazine assignments that will add to a meaningful body of work. It's not that there isn't work; there is. But it's often work without much depth; it's more about illustration. I'm not an illustrator and I don't want to be an illustrator. I want to make images that are profound. I am thinking about the great single images that we all remember—the photographic icons—I want to make a few of those in my lifetime.

The challenge now is to find the means to continue doing my work, to keep growing as an artist and to keep that inspiration alive. There are all sorts of levels of success. Nowadays, it seems that people have become addicted to fame—it's like a drug. For me, success is about doing great work—I want to be able to continue to do powerful and meaningful images.

BARBARA EDDY

....

The fifties have been a wonderful time for me; it's all been very positive. I think I was put through the experience of having cancer for a reason—and that reason was to help other people. My life is going to continue because I am doing something with that experience.

profile

When we take responsibility for our own lives, when we say there is a path to health we have to walk on, then we must know not only how to go forward, but what has brought us to this juncture.

DEENA METZGER, *Tree*

HER MEMORIES BEGIN FROM THE AGE OF SIX: stored as a kind of mnemonic of the soul—a psychic keepsake—is the image of a woman recumbent on her death bed, an open sore where her breast had once been. Forty years later, on Valentine's Day, the childhood remembrance exploded into a painful déjà vu as Barbara Eddy was told she had breast cancer. What must go through a woman's mind when she hears the words, "I'm sorry, the biopsy is positive"?

For Barbara it was the fear, "Am I going to have this sore that never heals? Am I going to die, too?" To this day she still doesn't know why her mother's incision didn't mend—"perhaps the malignancy had spread to her skin," she reasons—but her mother died shortly after the surgery, when she was only twenty-seven years old, leaving Barbara to be a six-year-old "woman of the house" for her father and younger brother.

Barbara Eddy is one of the one-in-eight women who are annually diagnosed with breast cancer. After a lifelong terror that she too would succumb to the same tragedy as her mother, Barbara has survived her bilateral mastectomy beyond the clinical timeframe of five years and stretched it into nine cancer-free years. But hubris is not a component of her character, and she still knocks on wood.

> The disease is in the conflict between the authentic inner voices and the external voices that fight against it. The mother-father-terror voices. The be-a-good-wife, the don't-divorce, the don't-quit-your-job, the don't-agitate, the don't-put-your-work-before-your-children voices, the be-a-good-neighbor-cook-housekeeper voices, the stay-with-the-man-you're-with voice, the financial-security voice, the don't-agitate voice, the don't-be-a-radical, don't-be-a-communist, don't-be-a-femi-nist voices, the don't-take-risks, don't-make-waves, do-fit-in-temper-assimilate-be-quiet voices . . .
> Cancer is silence.
>
> *Deena Metzger,* Tree

For the final ten years of her twenty-five-year marriage, Barbara lived in silence. "I never said no," she reflected sadly during our interview. "I didn't have a life with my first husband—I took care of him." She cleaned the house, cooked the food, washed and ironed the clothes, and entertained the guests in her household that included her husband and teenaged daughter, all in addition to her full-time job as a secretary at the local university in Boulder, Colorado, where she still lives today.

> Brugh Joy says, "Every disease is an obstruction of the soul." Everything must be re-examined, altered, transformed. What was simply unbearable before is now lethal. What was painful is deadly.
>
> *Deena Metzger,* Tree

When she and her family moved to Boulder from Chicago in 1967, they met the man who would be their new family doctor, Rich Eddy. With a youthful ebullience, Barbara admitted that she had immediately "fallen in love" with Dr. Eddy; and then demurred, "I thought he was the nicest, kindest man I'd ever met." Unbeknownst to them there was a future germinating between Barbara and her benevolent doctor. For nearly fifteen years, theirs was a professional relationship. Not until they had both (independently) left their respective spouses and met through a local choral group did they begin to develop a personal friendship. It was Rich, acting as her doctor, who found the lump on Barbara's breast. They were not yet married, and Barbara felt it an unjust twist of fate to be facing the possibility of death while in the throes of a new love, a new beginning.

> There are two questions I could ask: Who are the demons who live in the dark tissues and say, "die"? But I am tired of asking that question. I would like to know who are the spirits who live in the flesh and say, "live"?
>
> *Deena Metzger,* Tree

Barbara credits Rich with providing the solace, confidence, and unswerving optimism that helped to save her life. Some years after her mastectomy and a number of synchronistic events, she made the decision to contribute her experience by working with other women who had also lost a breast. She started a business, It's Me Again, which fits women with prostheses.

> I do not think the issue is snipping and cutting. I think the issue is the flow again. What we allow to continue to move through us; what we take in; what we are willing to give out. Those of us who live as though we were dikes, dams, fortifications, and those of us who can think of ourselves as water.
>
> *Deena Metzger,* Tree

Before a winter journey to Boulder, where I would be lecturing at the University of Colorado, I booked myself into a conveniently located and inexpensive bed and breakfast—lodgings I customarily use when I travel. The proprietor was Barbara Eddy. During my four-day stay, as we began to relate vignettes of our own biographies to each other, it became increasingly clear to me that I had met a simple, unassuming woman with a compelling story.

My week in Boulder happened to coincide with a rash of revelations by women who had undergone silicone gel breast implants—the count was up to 20,000 per year for reconstruction surgery after mastectomies, and another 100,000 per year for purely cosmetic reasons. According to these women, there were large numbers of contraindications relating to their breast surgery.

As I listened to National Public Radio and watched the "MacNeil-Lehrer News Hour," I was horrified by the increasing numbers of women who were disclosing physical symptoms attributed to silicone gel leaking into and polluting their bodies. (I saw this revelation as a metaphor for the pollution, the desecration of the body from which we all come—the Earth.) Severe fatigue, numbness of the outer extremities, migraine headaches, muscle and joint pain, breast hardening, and blood clots were some of the signs alerting and alarming these women—and the millions more with silicone breast implants who watched and listened and worried if they would be next.

> I reach for new openness. Nothing can be covered up again. Nothing can be masked or disguised. Under a silicone breast, a cancer can grow undetected.—They had promised her a new breast just as good as the old one. They had promised it, but they could not keep their promise.—I refuse reconstruction. I claim my body, such as it has become, as my own.
>
> *Deena Metzger,* Tree

Barbara (who, needless to say, feels fortunate never to have had implants herself) has counseled a good number of women and supported them in their decisions to face their doctors and have the implants removed. As one client told Barbara, "My doctor said, 'This is just a scare; you don't need to worry about it.' I told him, 'This is *my* body! I want them out! And I don't want to have to defend my position.'"

Perhaps her work is a gratuitous act of compassion and empathy. Perhaps it is a way of caring for herself, of healing herself over and over again, or of connecting with her long-dead mother. Whatever the reason, Barbara Eddy provides a much-needed service to a community of women extending well beyond the borders of Colorado and into Nevada, Wyoming, Kansas, even Oregon and Florida.

Toward the end of my stay in her nurturing home, Barbara admitted that she wanted to begin to write about her experience with cancer and what it has meant to her to be of some assistance and solace to other women. As I encouraged her to follow her inspiration, I again heard the words of Deena Metzger impelling her sisters who share the mark of the Amazon warrior (or any other life-threatening condition):

> Yes, write poems, women, write women, I continue to say.
> I do not know if it heals; I do not know if it cures, but I know it gives us our lives.

*I*WAS MARRIED FOR TWENTY-FIVE YEARS to my first husband and I never said no to him. I just did whatever he wanted me to do. I took care of the house, the yard, made his clothes, entertained his guests, whatever was needed. For about the last ten years, things didn't improve, and I started having a life of my own in order to save my sanity.

He would let me go off with friends to the movies or bicycling, but between us he made all the decisions and we always did what he wanted. At one point he went to England to give a lecture for two weeks, and I stayed home.

While he was away, I realized I didn't have a life with him—I took care of him. One evening at dinner, for the first time, I said, "Bob, I want you to spend more time with me. I feel there is something lacking in our marriage." He looked at me and said, "You are number three in line. I have my parents and my teaching to worry about, you're number three and I don't need anything more." I thought "Okay, I have given you my feelings so later you can't say that I didn't let you know. I'll give this six months' time and see what happens."

The night I eventually walked out of the house, he had said to me earlier, "Are you ever going to be happy again?" I told him I didn't know, that I was really struggling. It was all I could do to get dinner on the table. He sat down at the piano and started pounding away, playing faster and faster, and I thought, "I've got to get out of this environment or I will lose my mind." When he went out for a walk, I packed my bag and told my daughter, who was then in high school, that I was going to stay with a friend. Eventually, I helped him find an apartment and I moved back home and lived with my daughter. My husband harassed me for two years. I had to have restraining orders put on him to keep him from threatening me.

I'd gone in for my usual yearly checkup and Rich, who was still my doctor, discovered a lump. After his recommended mammogram came up negative, he said, "We'll just watch it," which is normal procedure.

Right about that time I separated from Bob, and Rich separated from his wife. Rich and I began talking outside of our professional relationship and then began to date. Neither of us were divorced yet, just separated. But it was clear that I had to get out of that marriage—ten years is long enough to be around a depressed person—and Rich had been very unhappy as well.

Because our relationship had changed, Rich decided he could no longer be my physician. He suggested I go to see a surgeon, but it was six months before I actually got around to making an appointment. I went in for what I thought was going to be a routine physical, but the doctor said, "Barbara, I feel two lumps. Don't you feel them?" I said, "No, my breasts are very dense." I was never able to feel any of the lumps. He immediately did a biopsy and, of course, it was positive, so we went ahead with the mastectomy. I discovered that I had cancer on Valentine's Day 1983. Before then I'd never had anything wrong with me.

Rich took this course of events quite hard and blamed himself, thinking, "What more could I have done? Here I am falling in love with this person who was my patient, and now she is diagnosed with cancer." We talked about it often because he was suffering inside. But I reminded him that he did what he should have done: sent me for a mammogram—which showed no cause for a biopsy at that point—and nothing else could have been done.

So I had my breast removed and underwent chemotherapy because one of my lymph nodes was affected. Let me tell you, chemotherapy is *not fun*. Some people are sicker than others, I happened to be one of the fortunate ones who just felt nauseated most of the time. I didn't vomit until the last visit to my oncologist.

Of course, the disease affected my relationship with Rich. When I felt well, we tried to go for walks or to the movies or plays—we tried to lead a normal life—but when I felt so sick during chemotherapy, many nights we basically just sat and held each other and cried. It was a very bonding time for us. Rich was convinced that together we would get through this. I naturally have a positive outlook on life, but I still needed positive reinforcement. Whereas, when I told my ex-husband I had cancer, he screamed into the phone, "You're not going to live. Ask that goddamn doctor friend of yours." He continued to harass me, adding to my ordeal. I now feel that living that kind of life for those ten years may have brought on the cancer.

The fear of cancer was something I had lived with all my life. At the age of twenty-one, I had my first biopsy. I guess in the back of my mind I knew it was a probability that this would happen—that the biopsies would not always continue to be benign. Still, when it was discovered that I had cancer, I was totally devastated. My preparation didn't make it any easier to accept. I thought, as one always does, I guess, when they discover they have cancer, "How long do I have to live?" I remember saying to my surgeon, "But I love Rich. Am I going to die?"

I went to a Living with Cancer seminar that was conducted by the wife of my oncologist, who'd also had breast surgery. Most of the women there were sicker than I was. That was a very depressing time for me, even though I was determined to put the cancer behind me. I ate saltine crackers all day; it was like being pregnant. And I continued to work at my secretarial job at the University of Colorado because I thought I *should* keep my mind busy.

My oncologist was a person who really couldn't talk to his patients; he would give me an injection and that would be the end of it. During my last visit to him, my head was wrapped in ice to try to keep the hair from falling out—which it did to a certain extent, but not completely. He said to me, "Barbara, did you lose your hair?" and I said, "But I've been coming to you for six months! *Yes,* I lost my hair. Why do you ask me that?" He said, "My wife is losing her hair, the cancer has reoccurred." It had been five years since she'd had breast cancer.

I remember I got up out of that chair, went to the sink and vomited, ran out of that place, and cried all the way home, thinking, "Is this the beginning or the end?" He was with his wife; he wasn't with me, his patient. Even though I understand his feelings, I will never forget that experience. It's like my husband of twenty-five years telling me I'm going to die; you don't erase those words. Here I was, my last treatment, and I thought, "Have I gone through all this chemotherapy for nothing?"

To this day if I don't feel well, my immediate reaction is, "Oh no, the cancer has reappeared somewhere." I don't really think about it, though, unless I'm not feeling well. Rich is so perceptive. He'll say, "Are you worried? Do you think the cancer is back?" If I say, "Yes," he'll encourage me to go for a checkup immediately. That's the best advice I can give to other women. If you don't *feel* well and you're scared the cancer has reoccurred, go to the doctor, no matter how foolish you may feel if he says there is nothing wrong with you. Do it for your peace of mind.

Six months after I finished my chemotherapy, at the suggestion of my internist and my surgeon, I had the other breast removed. They felt that because I had the preexisting condition—a fibrocystic breast—on that side as well, and because my mother had died at such an early age, it *could* appear, although the doctors said it might also reappear in my bones, or liver, etc.—not necessarily in the other breast. But I wanted to get on with my life, and felt at the time that I would always be wondering, "Is there a lump growing in that breast? Will I have to go through this all over again? Will I have to put Rich through this again?"

So I chose to have the second breast removed as well. It was a terrible time for me. My breasts were very sensitive, very much a part of me as a woman. Losing them was hard. But, oddly enough, many women come to me and say, "I wish they'd taken the other breast as well," which they won't do, of course, if there's no cause. The women feel it's easier to be fitted for a prosthesis, and they are relieved not to have to worry about the cancer showing up in the other breast.

I don't know why they didn't suggest the removal of the second breast when I had my first surgery. I've had other women tell me their doctor said up front, "We're going to take the other breast off as well, if that's okay with you, as a precautionary measure."

I had a modified radical mastectomy. A radical means they take a lot of the muscle—really cut into the muscle tissue; they don't do radicals anymore. I have a very flat chest now, it's not concave, which it would be if I'd had a radical. Oftentimes they'll do a lumpectomy—removing only the lump—but many women end up having a full mastectomy later. I don't know what is the best route to take. For me, I had to rely on the advice of my surgeons, whom I truly believed in, and I had my history to consider.

More and more people now are discussing breast cancer and mastectomies openly; it's a little easier for women than it was twenty or fifteen years ago. When I do speaking presentations, if it's appropriate, and almost daily with every fitting I do, I will open my blouse and show the woman my scar tissue and what my chest looks like so they have something to compare. That puts them at ease because they haven't seen another woman with a mastectomy.

My first prosthesis was very heavy—it was a huge bra that covered me from my chin to my tummy. Mastectomy bras are large and have a pocket where the prosthesis fits. I was a jogger at the time, and this thing was flopping up and down as I ran—I hated it. I wanted to be feminine even though I didn't have a breast; so I searched for two years to find something lighter weight.

Finally, one day, I found a prosthesis that was made out of foam rubber—it was really a bathing suit prosthesis. I said to the saleslady, "I'll take two of those. Anything's better than this heavy bean-bag I'm wearing." I wore them for four years and, in the meantime, had the other breast removed. Now I wasn't balancing the weight of one breast. After four years the foam rubber started to get lumpy because it's not really designed to be worn every day. When I returned to the same store, sure enough, it was out of business.

About that time Rich came home one day and said, "I have a patient who needs a prosthesis; can you help her?" I had a brochure from the company Nearly Me, which came with my prosthesis. And I thought, "How many bells have to go off before . . . ?" So I called California and spoke with the marketing rep at Nearly Me. I wanted to know if this was something I could do from my home. Their response was, "What better person than someone who has actually gone through this experience?"

The Nearly Me prostheses are a combination of silicone gel and foam rubber. No one else has this combination; they're all made only from silicone gel, that's what makes them heavy.

I started my own business, It's Me Again, in July 1989, and I have now seen well over four hundred women. I have them coming from New Mexico, Wyoming, Kansas, Nebraska. I've had calls from Oregon to Florida from other women, asking me how I got started and what they could do.

Eventually, I'd like to get more women who have had mastectomies to become home-fitters. There's no better person than someone who has walked in their shoes to understand what a woman goes through when she loses her breast. And to do it in the privacy of one's home; to me that's the only way to go. In the beginning I went from store to store trying to be fitted. It can be very embarrassing. I hear a lot of horror stories. It's such a rewarding experience for one who has gone through this surgery and experienced the fear of cancer to be able to help somebody else, because women don't know where to turn, they don't have a clue where to go.

All my life—from the time I was a young girl until I left my marriage in my mid-forties—I'd felt that I was unworthy, that I didn't have the smarts of other people. Finally, I found the strength to divorce my first husband and try something different. Many people stay in an unsatisfying marriage because it's easier, but I knew I was going down—feeling less and less useful. Now I feel the total opposite; even though I still have those tapes that say, "Well, you can't play bridge, so you're not as smart as other people." But I know that what I'm doing many people can't do. The bed and breakfast is a wonderful opportunity to communicate with people, to make them feel at home, to enjoy them.

I was a secretary all my life until after my cancer surgery. I always took orders from someone else. Now I've kind of blossomed into my own. *Yes,* I can do something. I *can* think for myself. I am out of that situation in which someone is telling me what to do. I have proven to myself through the success of my business that I do have some smarts. That feeling is very positive and rewarding. It's not an extension of anybody else. Nobody is telling me how to do anything or what to think; all the decisions are mine. No one makes *all* the right decisions, but I try to learn something from the experience when something happens that I'm not happy with. There are lessons to learn from everything that happens in one's life. I never thought this way before.

The fifties have been a wonderful time for me; it's all been very positive. I think I was put through the experience of having cancer for a reason—and that reason was to help other people. My life is going to continue because I am doing something with that experience. How long it will continue, nobody knows. Maybe I'm all wrong in feeling that way, but I don't think so. I know I'm a much stronger, more positive person now. Yes, I'm scared the cancer will reappear, but it's been nine years February 14, 1992. So the longer I'm free of it, the more I feel there is a plan for me—to go on and help other women.

I decided not to have silicone gel breast implants because I was going through such a traumatic time in my life already: I had cancer, I was dealing with a very paranoid, vindictive husband, I had lost my breasts, and I was falling in love with Rich. I thought, "I can't deal with one more thing right now." Also, my breasts had been very sensitive, and I was told there would be no sensitivity with implants. They are just a mound of silicone under the skin, and if you choose to have a nipple, that's a second surgery. And there was the possibility that they wouldn't look good and I wouldn't be happy with the end results. So I said, "I don't want any part of having something foreign in my body." Now, of course, there is a huge concern about the safety of silicone gel implants.

I am seeing more and more women who are choosing to have their implants removed. One woman came to me from Kansas. She had begun to lose the use of her right arm, but the doctors couldn't find anything wrong with her. No one made the connection. After a while she felt certain the implants were the cause of her numbness. She came to a doctor in Denver and, sure enough, they had been leaking and she immediately had them removed. How much of that silicone gel is in her body and where it goes, nobody can determine. I fitted her for a prosthesis on both sides. She sent another woman from the same town with the very same problem: leaking implants. That woman told me about a *third* lady in their town who is in a wheelchair as a result of her implants leaking. Now, that is their opinion, not their doctors'. Unfortunately, no one takes the opinion of the woman.

I had a striking young woman here recently who was not a cancer patient, she was a model. She'd had augmentation surgery to make her breasts the same size.

She told me one implant became very hard, that's what happens—the body protects itself from the foreign substance by forming scar tissue and pretty soon, it's inevitable, the implant becomes a hardened mass. This woman was bitter when she told me, "They said cigarette smoking did not cause cancer either."

She went to a plastic surgeon in town here, and his remark to her was, "How are things holding up? (Ha-ha.) This is just a scare; you don't need to worry about it. I'll put another one in." Her response was, "This is *my* body. I want them out. And I don't want to have to defend my position." So she had them removed.

Women don't know that when they have reconstruction surgery, their breast is basically cut off flat. It's a mound that has no shape to it, so oftentimes it won't fill out a bra cup. They come to me after the surgery and end up with a prosthesis after all. There is now an augmentation operation in which the skin is pulled up from the stomach and a breast is formed from the fatty tissue. This weakens the stomach muscles, plus being an eight-hour surgery—you are under the knife for *eight* hours! Some women are choosing to do this. Is it worth it? Recently, I was horrified to see a young girl on a television program say, "I don't care what happens; I'm going to have the implants." That's like sticking your head in the sand as far as I'm concerned. But I hope they come up with something safe so that women do have that option if they choose. For me, it was not the way I wanted to go, so I'm very flat-chested. At least I have something on the outside that's safe and I don't have to worry about it.

Before I decided to have the second breast off, I asked Rich what was his feeling about it. We were not married yet. He didn't want to tell me one way or the other what I should do, but he did say, "It's entirely up to you. Of course I would miss a breast, but I'm not marrying you for your breasts. I'm marrying you because I love you."

As I mentioned earlier, my breasts were very sensitive. When Rich touched my breasts, I was ready to roll! It's something I miss, but as time goes on, I forget about them. Obviously, I have very little sensation there anymore, but sensation is heightened in other parts of my body. Our sex life is certainly not impaired one bit. There really isn't anything missing as the result of my losing my breasts except they were there and they were sensitive and they were very much a part of my life—that I guess I do miss—but I don't think about it. I have so much else to be grateful for.

At first it was difficult to look in the mirror at myself because I looked like a little girl who had never developed. Someone once said, "You don't even have the raisins on a breadboard." After nine years I've learned to live with it. I still have a hard time going to public swimming pools and dressing in front of other people. I am conscious of the fact that I don't have breasts and maybe, as a caretaker, I'm more concerned about upsetting the other person than about myself.

One in eight women are now being diagnosed with breast cancer, and my goal is to help as many of those women as I possibly can. I don't necessarily want to promote my product; I want to promote the idea of the service. I don't care what prosthesis you buy; I want you to be fitted by someone who is caring. I don't want it to be an embarrassing situation.

Often women come to me with poorly fitting prostheses and I say, "Your natural breast doesn't even fit into this bra, why did you buy it?" But they tell me that was the size the saleslady said they should wear. It makes sense to work with what you already have. So when I fit a woman I make sure her natural breast fills that cup. Then I try to match it with the prosthesis, and will err on the small size. I tell them, "I will not make you look like Dolly Parton!" There's so much to this process, emotionally and physically—how they view themselves, how they feel about their bodies, how they feel about a missing breast.

I see the boundaries of my life as endless. I want to get involved with Earth Watch, to explore, to do more traveling. I want to reach out and help more people. How is this all going to happen? I don't know, I just have to let it happen and trust that if I'm not too structured and rigid that it will all come together as has my prosthesis business. I just think the years are going to get better, although I don't know how they can get any better than they are right now!

Since the cancer, my goal is to live every day to the fullest. I thank God for giving me this opportunity to be here today, for the people who are passing through my life, for living in this beautiful setting. Whenever the day is nice and birds are singing, I *hear* those sounds, I *see* the Flatirons, I *see* the clouds, the blue sky; maybe not every day, but I try to be thankful for my life and where it has brought me.

DR. SYLVIA EARLE

A century ago, if you lived to be fifty, you were old. You're not old at fifty anymore. Not at all. Some people get it in their brains that they're halfway, 50 percent; it's a nice round number to think you are going to live to be one hundred. And there's that increasing possibility, it's not a wild hope.

profile

Healing people and healing the planet are part of the same enterprise. People have a deep psychological need for contact with nature; the planet needs the reverential care of humans.

THEODORE ROSZAK, *The Voice of the Earth*

"I NEVER EAT ANYONE I KNOW PERSONALLY," said Dr. Sylvia Earle in a *New York Times Magazine* profile in 1991. "I wouldn't deliberately eat a grouper any more than I'd eat a cocker spaniel." A photograph showed Dr. Earle in full scuba gear wearing a purple wet suit with her arms protectively embracing a six-foot moray eel! By the end of the article, written by Peggy Orenstein, I was smitten with Sylvia Earle, who exuded a feisty spirit and an exceptional respect for life in all forms. She was appointed chief scientist at the National Oceanic and Atmospheric Administration (NOAA) in Washington, D.C.; and as one of the world's foremost divers, she had logged more than five thousand hours under the sea as an aquanaut and marine biologist.

More than a year after the article appeared, we met at her flora- and fauna-filled home on Skyline Boulevard in Oakland, California. Her thirteen-year-old black lab, Blue, seemed to add periodic vocal support to his mistress's remarks. No longer the chief scientist for NOAA, Sylvia spoke to me in her calming manner about many things—about being a woman scientist as well as a mother of three grown children and a grandmother, about the benefits of age, about her experience at NOAA as a government employee in the "private sector," about growing up with parents who encouraged their children to explore nature without limits, and about her love of nature, in particular the oceans of the world.

Sylvia's description of the ocean as a blue cathedral of water so clear that you can see sunlight streaming down forty or fifty meters below sea level is poetic and aesthetically irresistible. Sylvia makes no apologies for her emotional reaction to water. It is, for her, the reason for protecting and caring for the world's oceans (indeed, for all of nature): simply because they are "impossibly beautiful."

Human beings, she points out, protect works of art in museums and galleries. But why do we take for granted what might be styled as "works of God" or "works of Nature"? Why do we simplistically assume that "It's just a redwood tree" or "It's only another coral reef"? Sylvia hopes this cavalier treatment is at last changing—because, she maintains, the loss of these natural wild areas has accelerated to such a degree that by the time her grandchildren are grown, "Trying to find wilderness anywhere may be a very tough assignment."

Sylvia owes her own attraction to the natural world to growing up close to nature. She spent her childhood in New Jersey, where her family would spend vacations at the beach. As an adolescent, she and her family moved to Florida and her "backyard became the Gulf of Mexico." Her enchantment with the oceans began then. Her mother (who is still alive at ninety) was called the "Bird Lady," and children from throughout their neighborhood in Clearwater, near Tampa, would bring a steady stream of injured creatures, which her mother would nurse back to health. Sylvia is convinced that it was this hands-on encouragement to touch wild things that launched her into marine biology.

When war broke out in the Persian Gulf in early 1991, Sylvia, because of her title as "chief scientist," was one of the few privileged officials who traveled to the Middle East in order to view firsthand the decimation of land animals, sea creatures, and bird life. So far, she has made six trips to the area and written numerous articles, including one for the February 1992 issue of *National Geographic*. Sylvia described the devastation of natural life (which had previously sustained enormous flocks of resident and migratory birds—and people born in the "cradle of civilization") as one of "geological magnitude." As she spoke, I recalled the evocative photographs of the region I'd recently seen, taken by noted photojournalist Sebastiao Salgado: black-and-white scenes of men dwarfed by ruptured veins of the Earth and covered in a gossamer slick with toxicity. The sky was always midnight. There were no images of living animals.

Sylvia insists that all creatures, as well as the Earth itself, have their own kind of awareness. She told me of watching ants in the oil-covered Persian Gulf move clean sand grain-by-grain in order to cover the black crust caused by the oil spill. "It is obvious that animals wonder about things and are curious." But intelligence? "Whatever *that* is." She does not think it is necessarily good that a creature think like we do. And she reminded me that people think whales are wonderful because they are like us, and that dolphins are even more wonderful because they are *more* like us. "I think horseshoe crabs are wonderful because they're like horseshoe crabs! What's wonderful is the *way they* are, their variety and uniqueness," she said, her face animated by her enthusiasm. It should be clear, she feels, that as human beings we don't have all the answers; a lot of them are out there being worked out by all these other creatures.

Sylvia's love of the ocean is contagious. Shaking her head in disbelief, she says, "How anyone can know that deep-sea exploration exists and not just *burn* to jump in is beyond me." Thanks to Sylvia Earle, I had my first scuba diving class the next week.

THERE ARE LEVELS OF INVOLVEMENT WITH THE OCEAN. The best is being there, being there wet. Next best is being there dry on the other side of a pressure hole. The third best is to be up on the surface looking at equipment, and far behind that, as a last resort, is the procedure of using a net to blindly drag across the sea floor in order to bring up fragments. This is the traditional means of gaining information about what's down there.

There are the exciting discoveries that come with being out on the front line of exploration and research in the sea. Getting to know the ocean at night, above water and below, to dive down where no one has been before, to have encounters that are unique in human experience. I hope they don't stay unique; I hope they become part of the experience of all. We need to know what's going on, and if I can help convey that, it's another source of pleasure.

What's it like to be wet? Better than trying to describe it, I encourage people to go diving themselves. There is no substitute. Maybe by creating irresistible images—word images or otherwise—people will be tempted to do just that. I have always earnestly hoped that, if people get to know the place, they will care for it more. It's difficult to care for something you are not personally involved with. It's funny. We have a feeling of greater closeness to what we see from space, even looking at the moon, than we do about what goes on in the ocean or in a primeval forest. We are so captivated by the visual in terms of our approach to life.

We've been assiduously polluting the oceans and chopping down the forests. Battle raged recently on the grounds of spotted owls versus jobs. What a ridiculous cheapening of something really important, to create that nonsense. What we're talking about is the last remnant of Earth history that has been developing over 4.6 billion years. In our lifetime we can either respect and cherish it, enjoy and even derive economic gain from it—of a significant source forever—or we can chop it up and use it for toothpicks and paper towels and chairs, in a one-time orgy.

It's like, "Shall we enjoy the golden goose and benefit from the golden eggs, or shall we have one big roast goose and that's it?" We have opted for the roast goose—stupid, stupid us. We are doing the same thing in the ocean. That's why I went to Washington and that's why I left Washington. I went basically because I thought I could make a difference, and I left because I think I can make a bigger difference as a private citizen. As a little kid I was curious about the nature of life, the nature of what makes things tick, and the role of human beings in that scheme. As a scientist with that same curiosity—most good scientists, and I think I am a good scientist, retain that quality of childlike questioning—I haven't forgotten how to ask, "Why?" or "How?" or "What?" but especially "Why?" and even more, "Why not?" when confronted with an answer that is not satisfactory.

I don't think of the planet as a conscious organism as such, but I do think of it as a living system—that it is alive like a living creature. But then we can box ourselves in with words and open ourselves to gross misunderstandings and misinterpretations by others, who say, "Ho, ho, ho, what do you mean the planet that thinks?" Words might lead people to think, "What crazy direction are these loonies going in?" The system behaves as an interacting entity, as a whole—that's obvious. It is what it is: limited by its boundaries, the boundaries of the atmosphere, the boundaries of the depths of the ocean, the boundaries that we see surrounding this planet like an aura in space. It's here like a jewel, a *living* jewel. It's governed by chemistry, by physics, by biology; it's governed by things that cut across all of the more readily understood terms and concepts in the sciences. But, taken altogether, like the paints that go onto a canvas, something more than individual elements emerge, yet there is something that is even more than the image that comes with paints on the canvas. In the case of the Earth, you get something that is literally alive, and I have no apologies for saying that. It seems to me to be self-evident. It's more than just an abstract or physical process or series of processes. This is something that transcends the individual processes and becomes a synergistic effect of various processes coming together to make more than the sum of their individual elements.

For example, take the human body. If you look at a cadaver, all the elements are there, all the chemistry, all the physics of a human body—but you like to think a human being is more than that. I know for sure that a human being *is* more than just the lumps of protoplasm that constitute the structure and the organs that make us whatever it is we think we are. The planet, on a much more grand scale extrapolated from the same kind of concept, is much, much more than the physical particles that make up its structure.

The frightening thing, I think, is the rapid changes that we are witnessing in such a short period of time. My hope is that there is something I might be able to do with the knowledge I've gained in my lifetime that will serve to awaken people to what they've got, to protect it. Number one, because what right do we have to destroy it? And number two, our survival as a species is utterly dependent on the good health and continued functioning of the system as a healthy system, accommodating our presence here. If we mess it up, we do more than destroy a beautiful phenomenon in the universe or beyond. We destroy our source of livelihood, our ability to survive. It's the survival of our kind, our species. Life is resilient. There probably will continue to be life on Earth, no matter what human beings do. We can unleash horrible things like nuclear war, and certainly that's a valid concern.

I don't know what it's going to take for people to once again be close to the Earth, close to the sea, close to nature. We grow up in cities in increasingly larger numbers, and there's an arm's-length relationship with our roots. That's dangerous. It's not only sad that people lose that connection, it's really frightening. They become quite cavalier when they witness the treatment and destruction of the natural systems—perhaps with a tear in their collective eyes, but without fully appreciating that this mistreatment is doing something irrevocable and that it undermines our chances for survival. We *need* these natural systems; we cannot live independently from them. We have the illusion that we can package ourselves on some other planet with a handful of appropriately selected organisms that can supply us with food and the like. Maybe for a small number of people for a short period of time, that's realistic—we could take a camping trip into space. But it is pretty arrogant on our part to think we could create from scratch, replicate, something like what the planet is. I am very much a supporter of space exploration and space research and being pioneers into other realms, but for us to turn our backs on our own planet and not get it right here, to live within our environmental means, to strengthen harmony with nature, to do that first—if there has to be an either/or, this comes first.

Science isn't just about trying to find out how things work or what's going on, but also a sense of humility that is characteristic of many a fine scientist. Arrogance leads to thinking that you know it all, thinking that you've got the answers, that you can direct things. It's important to maintain this feeling of inquisitiveness, of humility, of questioning, of accepting that you will *never* know it all. Really good scientists, the best, know in their bones that finding an answer to one thing leads to sixteen more questions, then a hundred more, then a thousand more. That's part of the pleasure of being a scientist—you know you never get it all. That doesn't diminish in any sense the wonderful discoveries and breakthroughs in science and engineering, but the true heroes tend to be not those who are so carried away with their own self-importance and magnitude of what they have discovered, because it's an illusion, really it is. What new insights should provide is the perch from which you get to glimpse the magnitude of your ignorance and what remains to be known.

As far as why there are so few women scientists, I just say, "Give me one good reason why women shouldn't do anything they want to do in the sciences, engineering or math." There are no intellectual handicaps whatsoever. The barriers are truly there, but they exist because of culture, psychology, and social structure. Although the problems of the acceptance of women are certainly still there, and I see them every day, I am either bemused or frustrated with these attitudes and barriers. I'm pleased that I've come along at a time when I can enjoy my work in the sciences. I hope it doesn't close down in the future; I hope it expands because I think it's good for our species, not just for our society, to have women accorded the openness to be whatever they want to be.

I tend to be optimistic about life and the future and try to find the positive side to whatever is out there. Maybe I'm not focusing enough on problems that will drag us down no matter what. For instance, I'm very concerned about population expanding, and about diminishing resources. Our population is growing exponentially; our resources are finite. The planet is finite. We can't go on this way. It's just terrifying to think about the potential for disaster, and the disaster already existing.

The other side to this is that because we tend to live longer, we have more discretionary time. With luck, we'll be able to achieve a far greater proportion of the population that will be able to acquire those characteristics that we think of as wisdom. In China those who were able to attain the age of fifty, sixty, or seventy many years ago were really respected and honored. There still is that attitude in Oriental cultures generally, a tendency to show respect for those of greater age. We've lost it in this country. It *is* cause for great hope that people will live long enough to reflect on their experience and learn from that experience in the span of one lifetime. Now, in one lifetime, so much is happening so fast coupled with communication that enables us to see far more than any individuals prior to this generation were exposed to and could digest—well, let's hope that it gets digested.

I think wisdom is the cause for hope that we may actually get it right. Wisdom comes with age, although that's not a given, and some people, at a remarkably early point in their lives, acquire a wisdom, which isn't necessarily a reflection of intelligence. There's something that gives people special insight or lack of it, and it goes back perhaps to the attitude of humility, a willingness to pull back and look at the overview and not be so wrapped up in their own self-importance that they lose sight of where they are in the greater scheme of things.

When you think about it, when we arrive on the planet as a little human being, we have so much to learn. All the information we need isn't just naturally there in our brains; we have to learn it all from scratch. Certain emotions are there, but the awareness of how to cope has to be learned and learned and learned again. Maybe we're getting better at it through the increased forms of communication, at least we're getting better at certain kinds of information conveyance, but that's not a guarantee that it will bring us wisdom. We are getting an overview of information through the images brought to us from explorers, whether they are in the ocean or in the interior of a cell or in the space shuttle looking at the planet from afar. We have access to that great body of information; what we do with it, that's the trick we face right now. This is an opportunity special to this generation in that people will live long enough to knit the experience of their lifetime together—not just what is stuffed in their brains in school or what they get blitzed with on television. It's the sum total of their life experience that's on the line.

Especially when people reach that magical half-century mark. Decades seem to be turning points for people. Somehow, I have not really given much time nor thought to these decadal junctures, but I'm aware that it's a big deal for a lot of people. A century ago, if you lived to be fifty, you were old. You're not old at fifty anymore. Not at all. Some people get it in their brains that they're halfway, 50 percent; it's a nice round number to think you are going to live to be one hundred. And there is that increasing possibility, it's not a wild hope. It's expected that women, at least, will live into their late seventies or even early eighties. My mother is now ninety. People are not only living longer, they're in better health throughout their lives. We are gaining extraordinary insights into how to improve health even on a cellular level and conquer the cancers, the viral infections. I am confident that it will happen if we don't do something stupid to ourselves in the meantime and if we hold on to the life support system of our planet. I worry about those things, but I think I worry with good reason.

When you are in your fifties, you catch a glimpse that maybe time will run out for you; I certainly have caught a glimpse of that. There are certain things that I personally want to do aside from these other rapidly changing events that I have little to do with but feel strongly that I want to influence—causing people to be aware and to help set policies that would be more in tune with finding harmony with nature instead of this conquer-the-universe approach.

There are many women who expect to live another fifty or forty years after they've had their families, and say, "Okay, now I can get on with life. What do I want for *me?*" I hear this among some of my colleagues. It used to be a time of great trauma for women who have traditionally focused on managing families and the families go away: "Oh, the fledglings have left. Now what am I going to do?" they would ask, instead of embracing the time with great joy and thinking, "Now, at last, I can be me." Because there wasn't a "me" there for many, or at least they weren't encouraged to be themselves and not too many years ago it was rather expected that they would die anyway. Now I don't think a useful life is measured so much by reproductive capability—for male or female. It's nice to have daughters and sons; that is an obvious goal of living creatures, human beings included, but there's more to life than reproduction.

My fantasy of aging is that I'll have a rollicking good time, doing what I'm doing, continuing on as long as I can stay physically and mentally active. Mentally first. I just don't think about it all that much, except that I know time is finite and I want to take advantage to the best of my ability of the time I've got. But that's *always* been the way. It should be. You never know when the bolt of lightning is going to literally or figuratively come. You ought to live *every* day with the expectation that you're going to make the most out of it. That's what I've been doing and that's what I intend to continue to do. Anything else is just unthinkable.

I'm soon-to-become a single woman. My divorce will be final one of these days. But I'm not interested in being in relationship for the sake of being in relationship. I'm perfectly happy to be alone. I didn't seek out the last one, but it happened, and it was wonderful while it was wonderful, and when it wasn't, it wasn't. My soon-to-be ex-husband and I are still friends and do some work together. I can see how it could be otherwise for some people; it might not be healthy to continue with their relationship after a divorce. In this case, I think, it's just fine. There are things we don't talk about, things we don't do together, but some things we agree on and care about very much, and will continue to explore together. That's just fine.

I grew up in a time when people accepted, and I still harbor in my deepest philosophical self, the desirability of having a one-on-one relationship for life. That's my role model; my mother and my father were married for sixty years before my father died. They really *loved* each other and were so solid in a kind of magic that surrounded them. I had the expectation that *that's* the way it is, and I know it can be because I witnessed it all my life. It's a rude awakening to find that it isn't necessarily that way.

I've had my share of misfortune in my life. Who hasn't? I lost four brothers who I never knew. I consider that a substantial misfortune. There have been lots of small, medium, and large tragedies, but I tend to focus on the positive and not dwell on things that I could have done, or should have done, or things that happened to me which I wish hadn't happened to me. But rather, for every ten of those, I can think of ten more or fifty more or a hundred more that are really on the other side of things. You can drag yourself down wallowing in despair. I think it's a tragedy that all three of my marriages didn't work out. They have all been really tragic and stupid. We ought to have been able to get it right each time, but it didn't happen. It wasn't for lack of trying. Things are sometimes the way they are and you just accept it and get on with your life.

Success is all relative. I'm still striving for it. When you get one accomplishment behind you, you go on to the next two or three or six or ten projects. Once someone said to me, "Now that you've reached the pinnacle of your career . . ." I said, "What?" I still feel that way. There's so much to be done, so much that I feel I've just begun to start—just getting the tools assembled. Heavens no, I can't imagine ever getting to the point where I say, "Whew, I've done that. I'm finished." You are never really finished with anything, but you reach stages of putting things aside for a while and you reach a conclusion in terms of reaching deadlines or stopping points. But there's always so much more to do.

I think each person has to find their own purpose. Some people are purposeless, they spin their wheels and occupy space and consume resources. You wonder what they are doing here, and they probably wonder themselves if they ever wonder at all. My purpose is to have a good time, to try to be useful, to learn as much as I can, to convey as much of that learning—my insights and knowledge—as I can as a legacy to others. I feel compelled to give back as much as I can. It's such a gift to be here at all, to be alive—that alone, full-stop. And beyond that I'm very fortunate in countless ways: to have the family I have, to have the good health I've had, to have the ability to live during this time, to be able to travel and see the things I've seen, to do what I've done. To put all that in a big sack and, like Midas, continue to muse over the experiences is just so pointless. But to be able to take all of that and *make* something of it, to use it and give it back—that's the joy, that's the fun, that's the pleasure. I can't stop being a scientist any more than I can stop breathing. I will continue with first one and then another aspect of scientific endeavor, propelled by the curiosity, which is, "What next?"

ALLIE LIGHT

....

Meaningful work is what I care about now in my life; that's what my fifties have done for me. In my forties I was still trying to figure out how you get that meaningful work out in to the world. Now it seems quite possible to me.

profile

You're thinkin': How does a person know if they're crazy or not? Well, sometimes you
don't know. Sometimes you can go through life suspecting you are but never really
knowing for sure. Sometimes you know for sure 'cause you got so many people tellin'
you you're crazy that it's your word against everyone else's.
          JANE WAGNER, *The Search for Signs of Intelligent Life in the Universe*

"HOW MANY SOPRANOS DOES IT TAKE TO SING A HIGH C?" asked a woman at
a soprano tea party. She answers her own question with gusto, "It takes seven sopranos to sing a high C—one to sing it, and six to say they could have sung it better." Of course, the joke was on them, sopranos all, and they loved it. This is one
of many humorous, touching, and inspiring moments in the film *In the Shadow of
the Stars,* which won an Academy Award for best documentary feature in 1992.
Produced, directed, and edited by Allie Light and her husband, Irving Saraf, the
film was sensitively and compassionately produced, a celebration of talent and the
human spirit embodied by the choristers of the San Francisco Opera. It highlights
eleven individuals through interviews, dressing room and rehearsal shots, auditions,
performances, and visits at home, during which they discuss their careers, private
lives, and artistic aspirations. They represent the professional unsung heroes and
heroines of opera throughout the world, and through their candor we sense the
extent to which music has guided their lives and touched their souls.

The film was originally inspired as a tribute to (and is dedicated to) Charles Hilder,
Allie's first husband, who was a member of the chorus. Charles died in 1966 of
lymphoma. He had often carried an 8-millimeter camera under his costume and
filmed all the great stars on stage. More than two decades after his death, Allie and
Irving decided to incorporate the footage in a film about choristers. At the time
she felt it was a way of saying goodbye to the man she loved, although she now
admits, "The film has gone so many miles beyond just a desire to say goodbye to
my first husband. I'm grateful, because in that way it also extends his artistic life."

My first glimpse of Allie came on Monday, March 30, 1992, while watching the
Academy Awards. When the announcement was made for best documentary feature, up bolted a couple who have been together so long they have come to re-
semble each other. Irving, wearing a tuxedo, displayed an eager excitement that

was contagious; Allie seemed more subdued—as she is in person. However, when it came her turn to give an acceptance speech, she only managed to say, "Adío, Chas" before the cameras cut her off. I didn't know who "Chas" was, but I did know that this woman had been responsible for one of the most poignant moments during the presentation of the Academy Awards. It was Allie's very apparent integrity, her accomplishment, and her timorous nature that made me curious about her.

About a month later, we met at her home, a large Victorian house painted purple that sits on a hill in the Glen Park section of San Francisco. The house reflects the creative fervor of two filmmakers who have been part of an artistic community for decades. There are photographs everywhere, as well as paintings and books. And, of course, in a place of prominence on the mantel piece: two golden Oscars. One wall in the dining room was literally covered with notes of congratulations and mazaltov from friends from around the world.

Allie described to me her "experience of a lifetime" in Hollywood on the night of the Academy Awards. At the Dorothy Chandler Pavilion, she alighted from the limousine she and Irving had rented in order to allow four of their six children to accompany them. There were banks of cameras, famous stars, and a mile-long red carpet. How did it feel to make this kind of entrance? Allie assured me it was the most spectacular entrance she had ever made—except for the time she got arrested for protesting an embargo against Nicaragua. After the arrest she was taken in a paddy wagon to a jail, and when she stepped down from the vehicle, she was greeted with thunderous applause by her fellow protesters.

Allie operates on two assumptions: that art and politics cannot be separated—that the personal is political, and that if an artist doesn't start with the experiences from her own life, she is cheating. She remains true to these beliefs. When Allie was in her late twenties, she had a serious bout of depression that landed her in a psychiatric hospital, and she underwent psychoanalysis and antidepressant drug treatment. Decades later, in an attempt to find resolution and make peace with the stigma of this experience, she decided to make a documentary about women and their "madness." The film is called *Dialogues with MadWomen*. As Allie described her ordeal with doctors and hospitals, and how she had tried to be "as good a girl as I could be and it didn't work," I remembered a poem by the twelfth-century Persian poet Rumi and made a mental note to send her a copy:

> Conventional knowledge is death
> to our souls, and it is not really *ours*.
>
> We must become ignorant
> of what we've been taught,
> and be, instead, bewildered

Run from what's profitable and comfortable.
If you drink those liqueurs, you'll spill
the springwater of your real life.

Forget safety.
Live where you fear to live.
Destroy your reputation.
Be notorious.

I have tried prudent planning
long enough. From now
on, I'll be mad.

RUMI, "A Spider Playing in the House"
(in *Feeling the Shoulder of the Lion: Poetry and Teaching Stories of Rumi,*
Putney, VT: Threshold Books, 1991)

I WAS BORN IN 1935 IN A SMALL TOWN in Colorado known as the pinto bean center of the world. My father was a poor farmer, during the height of the Depression. He was about twenty years old and my mother was eighteen when they got married. They were literally being starved out because there was no way of making a living. My father was working for food rather than money.

Eventually, my father joined the Communist Party and was run out of this town for being a Communist. In 1937 he took his wife and kids and came to San Francisco because this seemed to be where the political fervor was. We got a cold-water flat south of Market, got on "relief" (the welfare of the time), and started a new life. I'm glad he did that. I would hate to have been raised in the small town where I was born.

World War II came along, and my father became a welder in the shipyards. We moved into the Sunnydale Housing Project when it first opened. I still re-member at age six how wonderful it was to move into this place, because it was clean, there was hot water, and everything was new.

When the war was over, we moved into a Mormon community in Utah. I was the only person in the high school who was not Mormon. There was a lot of peer pressure, but also I felt the need to belong. So I joined the Mormon church. My father was aghast. Here he was, a Communist who had left his fundamentalist upbringing—all his family were Pentecostals and Southern Bap-tists—and now his daughter was reverting back. I think it was a way of re-belling against my parents as much as anything else.

We lived there until I was sixteen, and then moved back to San Francisco, where I finished high school. I met my future husband through the Mormon church I attended, and we were married when I was eighteen. Charles was in college, he came from a working-class family and was considered the "differ-ent" one, just as I always felt different in my family. He was a singer and stud-ied music and voice, and later became an opera singer. As soon as we got married, we stopped being Mormons. That had been the place to meet and form our alliance.

Charles was drafted into the Korean War and spent two years at Ford Ord, California. My two oldest kids were born while he was in the Army. When he was discharged, we moved into a housing project, he went back to school to get his teaching credential, and I started dabbling around. I was always writing poetry and going to school, but really had no self-confidence or self-esteem (although those words weren't bandied around then). I lived through my husband; he was a charismatic, effervescent type of person, always up, always happy. I think I lived in a reflection of him.

My third child was born in 1960, so I had three children under the age of six. When I was twenty-seven, I had a breakdown. I got very depressed and began seeing a psychiatrist, who put me on a lot of medications that were not helpful. Finally, I committed myself to the day ward at Langley-Porter Psychiatric Institute, mainly because I was suicidal. I'm not sure what caused the breakdown. I can't really say that it was because I was not doing my thing, as people came to say later. Probably it was all the years of poverty; I felt I was repeating the life of my mother and her mother. Here we were, back in a project. At least I'd grown up and was no longer a helpless, oppressed child; supposedly, I was an adult. But I think it had to do with earlier insecurities and fears that looked like they were turning back on me again.

This happened to me before the Women's Movement began, and it's going to happen again to young women if we don't continue to support the Women's Movement and recognize that there are other options for women. But I didn't know that in the '60s. I was just this twenty-seven-year-old woman trying to figure out my life and raise three kids.

I think seeing a therapist helped me in the short run, but in the long run Freudian psychology is not good for women. There was a constant effort on the part of the male therapist to fit me back into what I was trying to get out of. That's part of what cracked me. I was trying to get out, and they were trying to shove me back in either with tranquilizers or antidepressants.

Soon after I was admitted to Langley-Porter, I was given a weekend off if I would go home and bake a turkey and scrub all the floors. Those are the kinds of assignments the psychiatrist gave me. I trusted that the doctors were doing their best to get me well, so I *did* bake the turkey, I *did* mop the floors. I did what they told me to do, but it still didn't make me well. I was as good a girl as I could be and it didn't work.

I spent three months there and was released, still depressed, and also very drugged—now I was taking Thorazine, Stelazine, Elavil. So I was probably worse off than I was before. Then the worst part of my life began: my husband got lymphoma and died in a very short time. I was just coming out of my depression when he developed cancer. I was not prepared in any sense of the word to take care of three kids by myself. Also, I was so identified with him that when he died, I thought that I had died. I just got under the covers in bed at my mother's house and stayed there, so they put me back in Langley-Porter. This time I was there day *and* night for about two or three weeks; it was a real crisis. I now know that I should have been allowed to cry, but every time I cried, they gave me a shot of Thorazine, which puts me out—period.

I remember telling the doctor, "I must be allergic to Thorazine, please don't give it to me because I go unconscious." He called the technician and they gave it to me right in his office, and the last thing I remember is that he was checking my eyes to see if they were dilated. Three days later, when I finally woke up, he said, "Well, we won't give you Thorazine again." Now I would say, "Why didn't you listen to me?" But at that time I couldn't stand up to them.

Some things that happened to me after Chas died are indicative of what can happen to a woman who really hasn't had freedom before. There was some part of me that took off like a bird in a way. I was mourning a lot, and I was struggling with these three kids. But also, something came awake in me. I'm not sure what it was—maybe a sense of identity. I began to think about what I might do with my life in a way I had never thought before. I always had let things happen to me. It *happened* that I got married; it *happened* that I got pregnant. So I think in order to combat that surging of independence and individuality, I got married again right away. That marriage didn't last very long, although I learned a lot from him. He was an artist as well as being an intellectual, a photographer. He built a darkroom and I began to take photographs and develop and print my own work. I was writing poetry throughout this period; it was the time during which I created my best work, and the poems were eventually published as *The Glittering Cave*.

The first time I actually made a choice in my life was when I told him he had to move out. I went back to school at San Francisco State and, for a year or so, I was without one man—there were many men in my life, but they passed in and out. I wasn't interested in having a relationship that would last. I think I went a little crazy; you can't do that now with AIDS around, but I had as many lovers as I wanted. I was very serious about school and I did very well—it had taken me eighteen years to get my BA in poetry and writing. And then I got into graduate school there in the interdisciplinary art department. I was really finding my way as an artist. Those were exciting years.

Then Irving and I got together. We've been together twenty-one years now. I've learned a tremendous amount from him. It was at the same time I met him that I was struck full force, right between the eyes, by feminism, by the Women's Movement and what it meant. I almost needed no description of what the Women's Movement was. The minute I heard it, I understood my life. It's not as though there were a lot of pat answers, but I understood what had been missing in my life. I strongly believe we have to keep the principles of feminism in the forefront because otherwise our daughters and their daughters are going to get lost again.

Feminism is a way of seeing the likeness of ourselves in other women—something I didn't have when I was in a psychiatric hospital. I had *no* idea other women felt as I did. Now I understand that they do, and they did, and they will. It's as if a community was there that was unknown and unseen to me, and finally surfaced. Judy Chicago said, "Feminism is the validation of other women's lives," and that's true, too. But first, it's the validation of one's own life, and once you understand something about yourself, you can understand other people better. In 1976 I coedited a book called *Poetry from Violence,* and I also began teaching at San Francisco State University in Women's Studies.

I became involved with a number of things that had to do with women at that time. One of them was the Women's Health Center. I felt like I was an older woman by then, I was thirty-four. I wanted to find out what it was like to do a cervical exam and see my body, but I had also heard these were all younger women and that sometimes they weren't too careful about how older women's bodies might be different. I didn't want to go there and feel hurt, so I thought to myself, "Maybe I'll make a film about the self-examination—that's a way of seeing myself, but in a safe way." That was the impetus to make my first film, *Self-Health.* It turned out to be tremendously successful.

After *Self-Health* Irving and I began to work together. He had made over a hundred films, but our first film together was *Mitsuye and Nellie;* then we did a series of five films about folk artists. Irving worked years for Saul Zaentz and for [public television station] KQED. I was teaching two or three courses a semester. As soon as Irving's three kids and one of mine finished college, we quit our jobs. We live purely as filmmakers now.

I've learned a lot from Irving, and he's done some important things for me. For example, after Chas died there was a memorial service for him at the Unitarian church; it was difficult because we weren't Unitarians—we weren't anything. I didn't know how to tell the children about their father's death, how to prepare them for life without him. Three months after he died, my oldest daughter thought his body was still in the hospital room; there hadn't been a funeral, we just called the mortician and they took the body away and that was it. All those years I never even knew where he was buried.

Twenty-five years went by, and then Irving's father died in Israel. I saw how the family was during the burial ceremony, it was a revelation to me. We went back a year later to Israel again, when they put the stone on the grave. I didn't understand before how important *some* kind of ritual is. In some sense I had never believed that Chas really died; I'd never allowed myself to do that. Irving said, "We're going to visit the cemetery." The day of the visit arrived, and my son and daughters came along. Irving had gotten flowers. I was scared to death. I didn't know where the plot was. We asked the caretaker and, with the help of a map, we found the grave site. There wasn't a stone, of course, because we hadn't bought one.

When we found the place on the map, I just fell apart. I fell down on the earth and spread the flowers all around; they were like tears and they fell everywhere. The kids cried; they were now the age their father had been when he died. It was the first time we came together as a family and said, "This man is dead; he's gone." Irving did that for us. Not only was he there for my kids all these years—he legally adopted them and became their father—but he made it possible for us to finally say goodbye to their first father. I'll appreciate it all my life.

I have a project called *Dialogues with MadWomen* that I will finish this year. It started because of my own experience. During all the years of my teaching women in the arts, I made a point every year to talk about myself and my bout of depression and breakdown. Always there are students who say, "I'm so glad you said that because it also happened to me," or "This happened to my mother," or "My grandmother killed herself because she was depressed"—it opens the way for women to talk about their lives.

I had always wanted to say where I was the day John Kennedy was shot—I was locked up in a mental hospital—and I could never tell people that. One day I decided that I was going to talk about my incarceration. It's really hard making that announcement in class or on the radio. Every time I do it, it's like doing it over again, because there's such a stigma attached to being in a mental hospital. It was such a relief for the women in my classes because they had the opportunity to tell me about themselves.

In 1988 I sat down and wrote this letter to a lot of friends, about a hundred people, and said, "I want you to know that I was in a mental hospital, and the time has come to make a video about it, and I need money. I'm asking everyone to send me $25—no more, because I think poor women should have as much input into this project as rich women, so I promise you I'll make something that will tell the truth." I got a thousand dollars or so back, which was the beginning of *Dialogues with MadWomen*. I was the first person I interviewed; it was the hardest thing I've had to do as an artist.

Then I met a woman at the Writers' Union, Karen Wong, who had been diagnosed schizophrenic (which was idiotic; she wasn't at all), and interviewed her. About a year later, she was murdered; somebody broke into her apartment. It had nothing to do with her history; it was just a murder-rapist who had stalked and killed her. I couldn't face those videotapes after that happened. For one year I cried over that senseless tragedy. I was so angry. Eventually, I had to look at the tapes, first with the sound off, then, gradually, I could listen to her voice. Now I'm in the process of finishing *MadWomen,* and it's going to be very powerful. There will be seven women in the film. I wish I could convince people out there making art and writing books, that if you don't start with your own life, you're cheating.

Irving's and my film *In the Shadow of the Stars* is another personal story, the story of Chas, my first husband, who was a chorister in the opera and wanted to be a star, but died before he achieved that. In a review of the film, a reviewer said, "Nobody could have ever devised what these people say in the film. The dialogue is too good." That's because it's their own stories. It wasn't written by us. We made it possible for this film to happen, and we put it together in such a way that it's miraculously edited. Irving is the person who knows how to edit, and I'm the one who sits there and says, "Why can't we do it this way?" "Why won't this work?" Then he'll go back and recut and it may work, or it may have been better before and he'll have to restore the cut. Irving and I have many other ideas. We always ask one another, "Do you think we'll live long enough to get through all the ideas we have?" I hope we don't get too old too fast. I feel that movies are our attempt to recover memories and dreams—to pull them back from the oblivion of unconsciousness. Jumpcuts are the minute performances of waking dreams—the personification of dream fragments in conscious life.

In terms of aging, my fifties have been dominated by menopause, and I think there really isn't any way for women to prepare for it. Hot flashes are very real! They are so uncomfortable, so regular, they sweep over you and you want to tear your clothes off. It's a very strong physical feeling. I think they started when I was about fifty-two, which was late, and I've had them for five years now, just about every forty minutes. They wake me up all night long. During the editing of *In the Shadow of the Stars,* I started timing them. I found that there is a connection between a brief feeling of despair, like what I went through when I was depressed in my twenties. It's the first time it occurred to me it could have been a chemical imbalance that was causing my depression. We don't hook the two together: this little moment of depression that hits so hard, fifteen or twenty seconds before the hot flash occurs.

It would mean a lot to me to know that over those years there could have been a chemical reason for depression, and I could stop blaming myself, my mother, and everyone for all the things that happened to me because I got depressed and fell into this pit. The last time I went in to have a pelvic exam, my gynecologist gave me some estrogen cream for dryness and I've used it. I read all the literature in the box and I think I'm going to drop it. I can't find one thing it's supposed to do for you and there are so many contraindications. I've gotten through menopause for five years now without taking estrogen, why start now?

Another important issue in my fifties is work. I think good, fulfilling work becomes more and more important. Meaningful work is what I care about now in my life; that's what my fifties have done for me. In my forties I was still trying to figure out how you get that meaningful work out in to the world. Now it seems quite possible to me. Those of us who have it are so lucky; and there are so few of us. During the fifties we begin to worry about how much longer we are going to be able to support ourselves or take care of ourselves. Something happens in the fifties; you begin to see that your dreams might not materialize, although there's a 90 percent side of me that says everything is still going to happen. And it *is* happening!

When I was very young, I thought it was okay to be female, but when I thought about getting old, I felt like I would want to be a man because old women were so ugly, unfeminine, useless, and of no value. One of the things that changed that attitude was reading about Georgia O'Keeffe and seeing what she looked like when she was old. She was so beautiful; she never became ugly; she just became more of herself and more beautiful. As a child I think I never had a very positive idea of what old age was. There was a poem I used to read in high school, in it a woman talked about her poor aging hands and remembered what they were like when she was young. That always brought my attention to the fact that my hands were going to get old. My mother has arthritic and very gnarled hands. I know that I won't have arthritis because her hands were already gnarled by the time she was my present age. I still look at my hands, that's where I see the aging.

I think the future is a continuation of delving down and in rather than out. The salvation for me all these years has been that every time something I do is either rejected or doesn't go where I think it will go, I think, "Just work, work is where life is." You go back to the typewriter or to the editing room. That's what I've always done, and I believe that's what I'll continue to do. If I don't have the time to work from the inside, what kind of life is that? It gives me a lot of pleasure.

My inner life is incredibly rich, it always has been. I don't need to be with people. If Irving goes away for three weeks, I can be here without seeing a soul. The last time that happened, I had trouble starting to talk again because I hadn't talked for three weeks. I absolutely love to be alone, maybe because so much of my life, I grew up in a housing project where there was never an opportunity to get away, to have the privacy that I value so much.

I think Irving gets lonely sometimes. He's much more outgoing, he likes lots of people around. When I force myself to go to a party, I always say to him, "Don't leave me, don't go away. Stay with me." I imagine that's how we all exit anyway; we have to realize that we can only die by ourselves. Death is going to happen to all of us when we grow up.

One of my favorite poems in *The Glittering Cave* is about my face aging. The book has silver mylar front and back covers and the poem is on the last page so the reader can look at herself in the mylar mirror of the back cover as she reads. I was thirty-eight when I wrote the poem, but it will always fit me and I just change the age in the poem as I age:

IN THE MIRROR IS THE GIRL WHO AGES

My face in the magnet mirror disembodied in a bowl of light
This round ocean on the wall my surface face floating there
pushing the sea asideskimming the air and light
and the submerged boneslungs burstingmove
  for 57 years toward the glass.
I've felt these bones in my chin seen the skeleton in my mouth.

And though fingers let go behind my faceI
thought the girl was still therecalled her back
under lightbulbsin daylight
bending her left to my right. I recognize our eyesher
name a cipher in a reflecting meadow her
invisible signature written backwardsmirror/wise.

DOLORES HUERTA

One thing I've learned as an organizer and activist is that having tremendous fears and anxieties is normal. It doesn't mean you should not do whatever is causing the anxiety; you should do it. By doing whatever causes your anxiety you overcome the fear, and strengthen your emotional, spiritual, activist muscles. But if you give in to your fear, you will never develop the psychical strength you need.

profile

No hay mal que por bien no venga.

SPANISH FOLK SAYING

"WHAT'S WRONG WITH THIS PICTURE?" thought Dolores Huerta one day in 1987 when she turned on the television set. "It's all men! Men who are the politicians and decision makers of America." She realized, then and there, the urgency for "gender balancing" in the U.S. political system and began to devote her time and considerable energy to convincing other women as well. Soon after that epiphany, Dolores spoke at a National Organization for Women conference at which she appealed to women to run for public office. This speech motivated former NOW president Eleanor Smeal, founder of the Fund for the Feminist Majority, to invite Dolores to be a board member of that group.

In the 1992 electoral campaign, an unprecedented 150 women candidates ran for the House of Representatives. The American media declared it "The Year of the Woman." Dolores Huerta's response was, "We are making it happen!" She is a woman who has been pivotal in making many things happen; she has demonstrated, picketed, organized, protested, lobbied, and mobilized for a variety of causes. She founded, along with Cesar Chavez, the United Farm Workers Union in California; she lobbied in Washington, D.C., for the Bill of Immigration, which would protect immigrant farm workers from deportation; she mobilized farm workers and consumers to force the U.S. government to ban certain pesticides such as DDT when it became obvious that these pesticides were poisoning our air, earth, and water, and tragically killing dozens of farm workers' children; she organized hundreds of strikes for farm workers against growers, and led many boycotts against a variety of agricultural products; in 1976 she marched on Washington in support of abortion rights in the case of *Roe v. Wade;* and, lest she have a moment to spare, she gave birth to and raised eleven children—primarily as a single mother.

Cesar Chavez marveled at Dolores for being "physically, spiritually, and psychologically fearless . . . absolutely" (Jacques E. Levy, *Cesar Chavez: Autobiography of La Causa,* New York: Norton, 1975). More than a decade after those words were spoken, Dolores was beaten unconscious (and nearly to her death) by San Francisco police during a demonstration against George Bush at the St. Francis Hotel during the 1988 campaign. In a few brief but savage moments, she lost fourteen pints of blood, had several ribs broken, and her spleen pulverized. But her spirit remained intact—"There is nothing bad, from which something good does not result," Dolores persuaded me, alluding to the Spanish saying by which she lives. "Every time we have had a major setback, our victories and gains have been a hundredfold more than they would be if we had continued at the same pace as before the setback. You don't lose faith because you see progress," she said quietly, her liquid eyes ancient and tired with all she has seen.

I met Dolores Huerta on Cinco de Mayo, a day of Mexican Independence. It was a fortuitous day to meet this most independent and courageous of women. Her daughter Lori had made the arrangements for our rendezvous at the apartment of another of Dolores's daughters, Juanita, who lives in a walk-up flat in the Mission district of San Francisco. Thematic posters addressing the rights of women and farm workers covered the walls, and political newspapers were strewn throughout the apartment—the influence of an activist mother, no doubt. For Dolores, it was a day like any other: up at dawn for an early morning interview on the Berkeley KPFA station to comment on the Rodney King verdict and the subsequent eruption of protest in South/Central Los Angeles; then back across the Bay to a late-morning press conference at San Francisco State University and a lunch with the Latino and African American faculty members; afterward she had lunch at a Cinco de Mayo rally; and now her appointment with me. After our interview she was whisked back across the Bay Bridge to Laney College, where she would again give a presentation; and that night, after her lecture, Dolores—no stay-at-home mom—would be going to a popular punk club in San Francisco with Juanita and other equally youthful friends. Are you tired yet?

Dolores and I sat in a sparsely furnished room with bare hardwood floors; our conversation echoed. She is an outspoken and intense woman, although physically small; and she sat in front of a stark white wall, recounting a life of intrigue and influence, speaking with the velocity of someone who still has much to complete in her day and in her life.

MY INFLUENCES HAVE BEEN GANDHI, Dr. Martin Luther King, Jr., and St. Francis. St. Francis said, "It is through giving that you receive; and through loving that you are loved." I learned from the example of Gandhi's life: he gave up his career as an attorney and lived the life of the people at the bottom of the caste in India. He proved that by sacrificing something you can accomplish greater things. I've seen that happen in my own experience.

There is nothing as hopeless as trying to start a union for farm workers. People said, "Are you nuts?"—and yet you see all that's been accomplished. It started with an idea and a first step. Now, with the Feminization of Power campaign, the dynamic is already in motion for political change.

I believe that things happen for a reason and that we are put in this life to make things happen. We're supposed to be working for change. What else is there to do? We're only given a few years to live on this earth, so we should do something besides feeding our face and acquiring a lot of material riches; we're here to improve life on this planet. The only decision we have to make is, "What am I going to do with my life and how can I make the world better for other people?" It's a gift and a blessing to be alive. Each of us is given certain gifts, and we have to use those gifts to help others.

That's my belief and what I try to teach my children—we're not here just to take up space or to be consumers of the world's resources, but to give back. I consider it a blessing to have the opportunity to work for change. For me, death is living in the suburbs—which might have been my life if I'd not had the opportunity to work in organizing. It's so much more exciting than living a middle-class life, having a nine-to-five job, and not being able to affect change. My life is like choosing the warrior's path: when you choose the path of the warrior, you can get beaten or shot at or even killed—that comes with the work.

My fifties were wonderful because many of my children graduated from college and my son graduated from medical school. Looking back on the years during which I raised them, I realized that I just *did* what I had to do. I didn't wait for things to happen. I used to take my kids along with me when I was organizing farm workers. I had a little Volkswagen, and I'd just throw the kids in the back seat. I always believed in involving them in whatever I did—that was by necessity because you just couldn't have a twenty-four-hour babysitter. As they grew older, and I started with the union, I'd take them to the picket lines. I took them to a boycott against grapes in New York City—they traveled all over the country with me. It was very rough on them.

Actually, the older ones helped a lot with the younger ones. My daughters Lori and Alicia helped the most. And, also, there was a space between the children because I was married and then divorced for a few years before I remarried. I divorced a second time and had another period without having more children. I never used birth control—my mother used to get so upset with me, even though she was more of a devout Catholic than I was. I just wanted to have children. And I don't regret that decision at all. I felt it was what I was supposed to do. And so I had eleven!

I raised most of my children as a single parent; consequently, I could do what I wanted with them—take them with me everywhere, they even went to jail with me. We were extremely poor, so poor that our clothes came from donations and secondhand clothing stores—in fact, secondhand-store clothes were a luxury for us! In the union we worked for five dollars a week at first, and later ten dollars a week and food stamps, then, eventually, we received a subsidy for food. The problem was that I was out of town so often I could never pick up the food stamps from the office! All my children were raised in a lifestyle of extreme deprivation—they didn't have clothes or toys.

My children are absolutely wonderful kids—they give me things and take care of *me*. Emilio is an attorney and I stay with him when I am in San Diego. He makes breakfast for me. I get embarrassed in public because they are so used to doing for themselves. They are just fantastic, all of them.

I had four children with my third partner, Richard. We started having hassles when our children were older. One of our daughters lived with her boyfriend in Los Angeles, and Richard was very upset about that. He wouldn't send her money or help her. Then another daughter decided she wanted to rent her own apartment, and he said, "These girls are just going to be out there free." I said, "I'd rather have them be whores than doormats." In other words, they weren't married to drug addicts or dependent on men in the traditional ways of Latina women. The girls are in college; if they have boyfriends, so what? Get real—it's the twentieth century. Richard and I have different lifestyles.

Sometimes you really care a lot about men and you want them to change. But at some point, after a few years, you think, "I don't really give a shit if you change or not; I'm just going to do my thing. If you want to hang around and keep me company fine." I don't know how many years I have left, but I figure I have to give what I can in my few years that remain, and not be worrying whether my old man is going to be there or not.

Many years ago I organized the first grape boycott, but nobody ever says I did. Then I came back and wrote and negotiated the contracts. Later, some young lawyers came in and wanted to change the history to his-story. Again, I was on the humble side of everything: you don't necessarily want credit or to have your name mentioned—that's not why you do the work. Still, it's a shock when you see the reverse happening—you are not only unrecognized for what you do, but you are *denigrated* for it.

In 1987 Eleanor Smeal, the former president of the National Organization for Women, started the Feminist Majority. She asked me to be on their board of directors after hearing me give a speech at a NOW conference where I talked about the fact that men are the decision-makers in our country. I told Ellie I would help her with the '92 election campaign. I've started the campaigns in Arizona, Colorado, and Washington state. I'm working to help women see themselves as public officials, and realize that they can win even if they don't have money, like Carol Moseley-Braun—she had $700 when she started. It's very exciting.

We have to start asking questions of the government. The message to the American public is, "Don't question authority." If you do you might get beaten or even killed. You can't ask, "Why spend so much money on an M-15 bomber—$4 billion—when we don't have money for schools or shelter or health care?" You can't question, "Where's the money from the savings and loans? Who's got it?" There is a militaristic, fascistic authority in power in this country right now.

I have big ambitions of things I'd still like to do. As women we need so many different things on so many different levels—like the raising of self-esteem—so that women can think more of themselves and not be so easily dominated by men or outer authority. We see this with young women and especially with Chicana women and other women of color, who have to deal with racial discrimination as well as the discrimination of being a woman.

We see a lot of pregnancies among our young Hispanic teenagers. Number one, they don't know how to resist, and number two, because of the influence of the Catholic church. We don't have the necessary dialogue on sexuality and birth control. It's easy for women to be dominated in a culture which teaches that they are supposed to be a man's servant.

I blame the church for a lot of the ills of society and the mind set of many of the Latino people. For example, many Latin men have the attitude, "I'm not going to get AIDS, so why use a condom," or "If God wants me to get AIDS, I'll get it." They have the mentality that you can't change your course of destiny. That sense of fatality and predestination comes from Catholicism.

Our primary need is a support system for women, which means that they have to establish that support system for each other. Networking, even down to the level of children—in grammar school and high school—is what we need. As Gloria Steinem says in her book *Revolution from Within,* "The more education you get, the less self-esteem you have." You are supposed to get an A+ for self-denigration. When minorities go to school, they learn so much information that is against their own culture. Not only do they learn it, but they have to prove they learned it by giving back the "facts" in examinations. We must fight racism and sexism at all levels. The closer you look at the system, the more veneers you see—the veneers of exploitation that exist against women.

I met a woman who is an attorney and a financial consultant. She has custody of her children, but she can't find a single judge in her state to enforce the custody order because her husband is the state's attorney general. So, it's not just poor women who are being exploited; they are women of *all* levels who are being discriminated against.

Another woman, Heidi Eisen, who was one of the first doctors to do research in nuclear medicine, wrote a paper on laser surgery. Another doctor stole her document word for word. She sued him for plagiarism and eventually won the lawsuit, but her lawyer didn't file for damages so she has to raise the money to pay the attorney's fees. When the university where she worked refused to rehire her, she had to file another lawsuit to get her position back and/or monies due to the loss of her position.

No matter where you turn, there is exploitation and a backlash as Susan Faludi's book says. I was at the women's march on Washington this year with close to 1 million women, but it only received a one- or two-day press coverage. That was it. Operation Desert Storm received national news coverage every single day, all day long for weeks. Before the march on Washington, the press was saying the Women's Movement was dead and, "Young women don't consider themselves feminists." Then, after the march, they announced, "The only people there were young women." They don't know *what* to say!

Women have to start making demands and taking responsibility because, as Frederick Douglass said, "You don't get anything without making demands." Nothing is given to you, you have to fight for everything. And it begins with families, in the home. We can't wait for men to change the way they act toward us. We can't wait for the world to change. *We* have to initiate the changes, to exert the pressure to make change happen.

I think the main thing is that women have to take responsibility as decision-makers in their families without fear. Even *with* fear, they have to be able to walk away from their marriage if their husbands won't change. The decision has to be made for ourselves and our children, and for our communities and the world. The world is not going to get better unless women make it happen. I firmly believe that. Women have a different type of energy—they *give* power, they empower; men have power over. Unless power is shared, it becomes corrupt.

Women need to have confidence and faith in themselves that we can find the right answers. There is a tee-shirt I like that says, "Behind every successful woman is herself." We gain confidence by doing things that we normally might not do—the things we're afraid of doing. One thing I've learned as an organizer and activist is that having these tremendous fears and anxieties inside of you is normal, it's natural. It doesn't mean you should not do whatever is causing the anxiety; you should *do* it. By doing whatever is causing your anxiety you overcome the fear, and then you strengthen your emotional, spiritual, activist muscles. But if you give in to your fear, you will never develop the psychical strength you need.

Young women—maybe they were lettuce workers—used to call me and cry, "I'm really afraid to strike." I'd say, "It's good that you're afraid. If you weren't there would be something wrong with you!" I realized that after I was beaten up in San Francisco, I had much more emotional strength than I had before the beating.

When my daughter Juanita was three years old she was walking in and out of the room where I was holding a boycott training session. Later, she was talking on her toy phone. I said, "Juanita, what do you talk about when you call people? Are you telling them to come and picket?" She said, "They're not ready for picketing; I'm just asking them to leaflet." At three years old, she was able to understand that you have to bring people along at different levels.

In terms of aging, when you first hit thirty, you think you are ancient, and then you get to be forty and say, "Well, I'm not so old after all." By the time you are fifty, you still feel great and think, "I should be old but I don't *feel* old." You know that eventually it will catch up with you—age is just a lessening of energy and you can no longer control what's happening to your body—it's going to happen regardless of what you do. I know that I will have to slow down some day, because I've seen it happen to other people. When I do reach that point, I'll be able to read books and do a different kind of activity. Right now I'm blessed to be able to sustain my pace and continue to do what I'm doing. I'll just keep going as long as I can and die with my boots on, I hope.

GLORIA STEINEM

Actually, aging, after fifty, is an exciting new period; it is another country. Just as it's exciting and interesting to be an adolescent after having been a child, or a young adult after having been an adolescent. I like it. It's another stage of life after you're finished with this crazy female role.

profile

IT WAS THE END OF JULY AND I WAS ON MY WAY TO NEW YORK, where I would meet Gloria Steinem. Her assistant had told me, "Gloria wants to take you to lunch." "Wow! Lunch with Gloria Steinem," I'd thought to myself.

On the day of our meeting, I arrived an hour early at the Park Avenue offices of *Ms.* magazine: I knew that the National Organization for Women had sent a film crew to interview Gloria about the beginning of *Ms.,* and thought it might be interesting to observe the taping. The still photographer for the day was a young man named Elvis, and to pass the time, we exchanged information about cameras and photography.

Cristina, Gloria's assistant, apologized several times to me and the NOW group for Gloria's delayed arrival. This show of concern was a sign of the enormous and sincere consideration Gloria shows toward everyone in her circle. It was a gesture I would witness countless times during the next several hours we would spend together.

Finally, the moment we had been awaiting: Gloria's entrance. As well-recognized a public figure as Gloria Steinem may be, she is equally unpretentious and unassuming. She made the round of introductions and again apologized for her delay. She looked as tall, blond, and thin in person as she had in the many photographs in which I'd seen her during the past two decades. And she still wears oversized glasses, though no longer the "aviator" shape you may remember. At fifty-eight she will soon be saying, "This is what *sixty* looks like."

On a bright but humid day in the middle of summer, Gloria wore black: a black short-sleeved tank top from which her collarbone protruded, black jeans, and a black belt. The multiple silver bracelets that softly jangled on her left wrist, accenting her long, graceful hands, were a symbolic political statement—each one commemorates a woman who died from an illegal abortion before abortion became legal in the United States. Her sandals were tan-colored, flat-heeled, but beaded and sexy. Always ready with a joke (often at her own expense), I overheard her tell one young woman—a member of the film crew in her early twenties, who was wearing shoes that were a close rendition of army boots: "How lucky, you're from the generation of comfortable shoes. I haven't liberated myself from the curse of uncomfortable shoes yet!" Exuding a kind of casual chic, one suspects Gloria Steinem could wear *anything* and still look splendid.

Her book *Revolution from Within, A Book of Self-Esteem*—which has had a long stint on the *New York Times* bestseller list—is a synthesis of history, politics, psychology, science, cultural anthropology, New Age experimentation, and personal exploration—all as part of a feminist worldview. The book is highly accessible to its readers. It came to be written, Gloria says, when she realized that even after all of her external liberation, she lacked a core belief in herself and a sense of internal reality. Several crises in her life—the severe financial difficulties and near-demise of *Ms.,* finding herself in the wrong relationship, and the sudden diagnosis of breast cancer—all precipitated the personal journey that the writing of this book necessitated. *Revolution from Within* has struck a chord among women who are struggling for self-esteem in a woman-hating society. It offers a simple answer—the development of self-esteem—without being simplistic.

In a crowded, noisy restaurant in what was then the Pan Am building, Gloria discussed why women so often only become themselves after fifty, why so many women grow more radical with age and so many men more conservative, why we *all* need to "come out" as our authentic selves, how menopause has freed her mind from an obsession with sex, and how "dreams are a form of planning"—for if our dreams were not already within us, we could not dream them. Her concern is for the ecology of the soul as well as the ecology of the planet, and she understands that a human being cannot be whole without honoring both.

I especially appreciated her inviting manner: she put me immediately at ease with her humor, kindness, and open friendliness. Our sense of complicity lay in the plain fact that we were women. In an outburst of my usual unbridled enthusiasm, I threw my arms upward and said, "I can't believe I'm having lunch with Gloria Steinem!" My scarlet face screamed my embarrassment at this spontaneous outburst. Then we looked at each other and laughed. Gloria said, "Well, *I'm* having lunch with Cathleen Rountree!"

Thanks, Gloria.

CAROL GILLIGAN HAS DONE RESEARCH ON WHAT HAPPENS to preadolescent girls when they turn eleven, and Carolyn Heilbrun has written about women "becoming themselves" after fifty. According to their theory, we learn to become female impersonators around adolescence, and don't become free again until after menopause. That means until the so-called "feminine role" descends upon us like an Iron Maiden, we are likely to be autonomous and strong, to know what we think and what we want as little girls. The role of female impersonator doesn't lift again (hopefully that will change) until the time we turn fifty. In some ways one of the best indicators of who we will be—or could be—after we are fifty is who we were before we were twelve. It's very helpful for older women to work with young girls for that reason. It's a good exchange. The Ms. Foundation for Women has many national initiatives for young girls, a variety of programs that try to strengthen, as Carol Gilligan says, "the healthy rebellion" in little girls. It helps young girls to not lose themselves when this role descends. They may have to adjust to that role—we all do to some extent—but they can have a double vision that includes their real self and know that it's okay to retain that self along with the other more socialized self.

This is the difficulty that Marilyn Monroe had during her lifetime: she had so little true self that she hid behind the role of a female impersonator, and she was idolized, for the most part, by adult males. What's different about the myth of Marilyn Monroe now is that since the Women's Movement began, she has been focused on by women because many of us saw her as so vulnerable and victimized that it was frightening to watch. Now, I think two things have happened: because of the Women's Movement, we're beginning to ask ourselves, "What if?" If there had been a Women's Movement during her lifetime, could it have saved her? That's intimately fascinating to women because it's saving a part of ourselves as well. In a way, her audience has doubled. It used to be mostly men; now it's at least equally women, if not more.

The second part of that is: some younger women, like Madonna, have come along and taken the symbols of Marilyn, which were the hair, the clothes, the simpering style—everything that meant victim and vulnerability— and used them with strength and control. It's no accident that Marilyn's fans during her lifetime were mostly men, and Madonna's fans are mostly teenaged girls. They're so vulnerable and needful of seeing somebody who is sexual and *not* a victim. I'm not saying Madonna is the *goal,* but she is a step forward. Madonna is in control of her art and her business, she's not humiliated—she's her own person. Marilyn made millions for other people, and she almost never had any money, she was victimized by many people.

During my mid-life I've gone through stages, and probably there are many more to come. My first response to aging was total defiance: "Fuck them! I'm going to continue to do everything in my life the way I've always done it." I didn't really begin to feel my aging until I was fifty, because I didn't have the markers of the passage of time like children or illness to remind me. I felt exactly like the same person I'd always been, so turning fifty was my first intimation of mortality. My response was, "I'm going to wear the same clothes I've always worn. I'll be the Ruth Gordon of my generation." She was wearing miniskirts when she was eighty-five and making the movie *Harold and Maude*. There is some sense in which what is conformist at twenty or thirty is rebellious at fifty or sixty. But in the end, that's just clinging to old habits.

A lot of things were changing for me during my early fifties: I was leaving an eight- or nine-year relationship with one man and transitioning into a new relationship; *Ms.* magazine, which had been my family and my primary commitment for the last fifteen years or so, was hugely and unfairly in debt; and, when I was fifty-two, I was diagnosed with breast cancer. I was so tired and at such a stopping place in my life. I thought, "Well, this is how it's going to end." If I had a recurrence now, I would be very angry, but then I thought it was a natural stopping place, because I knew I couldn't keep going at the same pace. Even so, I did all the research on cancer and changed my diet and got the right treatment. I certainly never wanted to die, but it seemed sort of appropriate. It was a way of resting.

I had a lumpectomy and radiation. It's been six years. It's great, but it doesn't mean anything. When you look at the breast cancer statistics, when they speak of survival rates, they only mean five years. It doesn't mean you won't have a recurrence in year seven or ten. They don't know; we just have to figure it out for ourselves, and realize that 70 or 80 percent of all cancer is due to diet and environmental dangers.

All of these things converged, and for the first time in my adult life, I had a crisis of my own making. Up to that time, all my crises had been of other people's making: my mother, the movement, the magazine. But this was just me. It was very hard. All the color went out of me. Now I know it is a common sign of depression. It was like the world had become black and white instead of color. The crisis forced me to stop and look inward for the first time. All of my life I had successfully been running from my childhood without realizing I was sometimes replicating it. I had spent a lot of my childhood looking after an invalid mother, and so I had turned the magazine into my mother. Also, I had never made a real home for myself—it's hard to make something when you've never had the experience of it before.

Gradually, I started to come out the other end and to recognize the fact that I had been repeating patterns I learned in my childhood. Once I realized where they were coming from and saw they weren't inevitable in the present, I was less likely to repeat them. I began to find pleasure in staying home, and I made all the changes in my life that sound so simple. From that experience I learned that to be defiant about age may be better than despair—it's energizing—but it is not progress. Actually, after fifty, aging can become an exciting new period; it is another country. Just as it's exciting to be an adolescent after having been a child, or to be a young adult after having been an adolescent. I like it. It's another stage of life after you're finished with this crazy female role.

Mostly, it's a feeling of freedom to do what you want to do instead of what you have to do. For me, it's the belated ability to occasionally ask, "What do I want to do?" as opposed to, "What needs doing?" Hopefully, that's something women will always ask themselves in the future, but for many of us—especially those who were trained to be 1950s women—it takes a lot of unlearning.

For me as an individual, aging has also brought freedom from romance; freedom from the ways in which your hormones distort your judgment and make you do things that aren't right for you. When I was younger, there was a part of my brain back here that was always thinking about sex. I might not have always been tending to it, but every time I turned around, it would be there. Sometimes it took over, sometimes I forgot about it, but it was there. It's not there anymore! It's funny—it's like you have an entire part of your brain that's free for other things. Going through menopause makes the difference. If someone would have told me this at forty-five, not only would I not have believed it, I wouldn't have *wanted* to believe it. All I can tell you is: it's wonderful. It doesn't mean you don't enjoy having sex when it happens, just that you don't *think* about it when it doesn't. It was wonderful before—I'm not knocking it—although I do think I confused sex with friendship, love, affection, and aerobics all in one. I could have substituted aerobics for some of it. It isn't that I regret the past, but it's equally wonderful now in a different way. To young women I can only say, "Don't worry about it!"

I never missed having children. I recognized the reasons why I didn't, and I realized it had a lot to do with the injustice in society. I'd seen my mother as a poor woman, alone, with a child, without money, without a life—it shouldn't have been, but it was in front of my eyes my entire childhood, and often in the world in general, too. I don't remember seeing women who had children and who were free. It was a choice I should not have had to make, but given what was possible in my life, I was much happier not to have children.

I only realized that I might otherwise have felt differently about it when, during my late forties (or whenever I was approaching the end of my childbearing years), one of my friends in India kept saying, "Why don't you come to India and have a baby here?" There were wonderful traditions that were part of a woman's extended family and culture: the mother lives in a household with a lot of people in it, she gets massages every day, for the first three months the baby is taken care of by members of the extended family—there is a whole Hindu ritual and support system. Suddenly, for the first time in my life, it began to sound sort of interesting. I realized only then that the conditions of mothering and childbirth in America obviously had a lot to do with my choice. But I never regretted it. I also don't believe biology means very much. I think children learn to love us and we love them, whether we're related or not. Now I have three young women in my life—one especially, who is my god-daughter and lives with me every summer—and that is enormously satisfying to me. I missed the experience of childbirth, but many women I know don't remember it anyway.

One of the great culprits in addition to patriarchy itself—though the right wing is busily blaming women in the work force—is the nuclear family. Before there were just two parents, there was an extended family system. If your mother was crazy, you had a grandmother, an aunt or uncle, or somebody. If you didn't share interests with your parents, you could find someone else. That possibility is gone.

The best example we who are over fifty can set for our younger sisters is to live the most full lives we can because only that vision—women who are really doing it—will help them to be themselves, too. Those women will do it better because we are still struggling with issues they won't have to struggle with. But at least we will have given some proof that there is a whole new country after fifty.

When I was writing *Revolution from Within,* it occurred to me that dreaming is a form of planning. If our dreams weren't already inside us, we couldn't ever dream them. We couldn't even imagine them. The question is, how did they get there? I never thought of it that way because, I think, until I got older, I had never believed in my own reality. I believed that I was what I did for other people, or that I was only alive if I was being useful. I've discovered this is a very common problem of women who are raised to be caretakers and of neglected children. Because you weren't focused on, you come to believe you are invisible. It took a long time for me to trust my own dreams as being inside me and real.

We all have the full circle of human qualities, but we have them in a unique combination that could never happen again. Just the combination of genes, environment, culture, and parents—it could never happen again, by definition. That means this unique self is already in there. This unique, true self speaks in various ways. One way is the joy and spontaneity in what you do. If you listen to that, let it guide you, then you really develop and nourish what's in there already, as opposed to imitating others. The moment we start imitating, we start being insecure because we can't be somebody else. It just doesn't work. It's hard to listen to this voice sometimes, because it's so challenging and subversive to outside authority. We spend an awful lot of time unlearning this outside authority and getting back to this basic inner voice.

It's true that almost everything in our society is against being authentic. But it's also true that it's impossible to live and be unauthentic. You can't be someone else. There's a parallel with what happens to women when we realize being good girls doesn't work—so we might as well be whoever the hell we are. It may take time—that's okay, we have to learn from experience. That's why older women tend to be more radical and activist than younger ones.

Women tend to become more radical with age and men tend to become more conservative. Patriarchies value women when they are young, sexual, have childbearing capabilities, and are energetic workers. If we have any social power at all, it's when we are younger; it diminishes as we get older, and we become more radical as we see our problems more clearly. Men tend to be the other way around; they have less power at eighteen or twenty, and then get older and replace their fathers.

It's interesting what is going to happen in this society, because the red hot center of the transformation of feminism has always been more likely to come from older women—not over fifty necessarily, but at least women who were in the labor force or who had kids and began to see what was wrong and decided to become active. Because knowing what's wrong and having the freedom to defy it tend to come even more with age, the fact that we'll have a bigger than ever critical mass of women over fifty in society is very fortunate and extremely interesting—it's really the future. Gerda Lerner, the feminist historian, tells me that such a critical mass of older women—who have some tradition of rebellion and independence and some modicum of security (not much, God knows), or at least some way of making a living—has never occurred before. And precisely because we ourselves have refused to have children to the same degree we used to, we are now a larger proportion of the population.

We need to begin treating ourselves as well as we treat other people. That would be an *enormous* revolution. Some of us, like me, for instance, took our female socialization and instead of putting ourselves into a man and children, put ourselves into other women; and this helped us, too, but we overdid it at the peril of health, life, and limb. In order just to survive and not die or burn out, we have to treat ourselves as well as we treat other people. We have to realize that being a Superwoman—the two-job syndrome, which was always a problem for poor women in this country, is now a middle-class problem, too—is just impossible. Until men are equal *inside* the home, women can't be equal outside it. It just doesn't work. I still don't see many women who have the strength and courage of entitlement to say to a prospective father, "If I'm going to have to raise this child alone, I'm not having it," or "If you want to

have a child, you're going to have to take care of this child as an infant, too."
It's not a punishment; it's a gift. I still think that, next to reproductive rights,
health care, and simple physical, bodily survival, the double role problem is the
biggest one for the largest number of women.

We act immorally the moment we begin to think things like, "If I don't do
this, someone else will, so what does it matter?" or "It doesn't matter what I
do, the world will go on just the same anyway." But if we say to ourselves as
best we can about each action, "This does matter," then we use each action as
a vessel for our best intentions. Even the most hard-nosed physicist is beginning to admit that the flap of a butterfly's wings in one place can change the
weather thousands of miles away. Everything we do matters.

COELEEN KIEBERT

....

I don't think of myself as a middle-aged woman. Sometimes I think it's time I start! Often I think I should be acting differently, or feeling differently, or dressing differently. When I'm shopping for clothes, I realize it would be ridiculous for me to dress in certain ways. But I just don't think of myself as being "older." I've heard people who are much older than me, whose bodies have moved further down the road of deterioration, say that they still feel very young inside. I understand what they are talking about.

profile

ONE EVENING IN THE EARLY 1950S, when Coeleen Kiebert was eighteen, her mother announced at dinner, "I've gotten a job, and Coeleen is going to the university!" Coeleen was the first in her family to receive a college education, and it was only because her mother took a stand and—against her father's wishes—went to work. Even though they were a middle-class family and needed the money, convention dictated that women simply did not work outside the home. Husbands considered this action an affront to their ability to provide for their families.

Coeleen remembers that her mother, who was a superb seamstress, was dressed especially well that night. Mrs. Kiebert continued, "Yes, I went downtown today and was hired at Amluxsen's," a high-class imported fabric store in Minneapolis.

"My mother had a highly developed aesthetic sense, a great gift for detail, and was an elegant, beautiful woman," Coeleen said as she recalled the following conversation, which took place over forty years ago. "My father asked, 'Well, is it a part-time job?'

"'No, it's full time, but I have Tuesdays off for bridge club.'

"'Do you start next month?' I loved this line—she didn't know how to drive:

"'No, I'll start tomorrow if you'll give me a ride.' So he drove her to work and picked her up every day for years."

Mrs. Kiebert quickly succeeded in the company and was highly regarded. But, more important, she showed something of great magnitude to her daughter that day when she decided to go to work: the fundamental feminist principle that a woman's independence can be derived through work and financial security, and the idea that work could be creative and fulfilling. Coeleen never forgot these truths.

After four years at the University of Minnesota, Coeleen graduated with a B.S. degree. She got married immediately, and after getting married, "immediately got pregnant!" In the early '60s, after reading Betty Friedan's, *The Feminine Mystique,* Coeleen forged a path for herself and her friends toward feminism, to which she has remained faithful.

The most striking quality about Coeleen is that her life is of a piece. As an artist, therapist, teacher, community leader, and friend, she places no visible distinctions between these ways of being in the world. Every aspect of her life benefits from her highly developed aesthetic sensibility: she has a sharp eye and a great gift for detail. Along with an admirable confidence in her own talents and a conviction in her beliefs, she carries the cool, calm characteristic often associated with her Dutch ancestry, just as she bares its external attributes: natural blond hair and the fairest skin. Coeleen's simple description of her mother fits herself as well: "a very elegant, beautiful woman."

The organic nature of creativity has been Coeleen's major focus in her own artistic work, in her therapeutic work with clients, and in her teaching art to students. Her theory is that creativity has been unnecessarily shrouded in an impenetrable mystique that makes it available only to a select few. Instead, she believes "creativity is a 'given commodity' that we all have," and that it can "bring joy and wholeness to our lives." Coeleen explores the psychological stages of creating in her self-published booklet, *All of a Sudden: The Creative Process,* as well as in her classes. It is her premise that shifting the focus of attention away from the finished product of an endeavor and back to the ongoing process carries with it an inherently healing capacity.

Coeleen's property, located in a quaint seaside village where she settled in the late 1960s, sits aristocratically on a cliff overlooking the Pacific Ocean. The 180-degree view from this "point" is breathtaking and gives one the sense (even if illusionary) of unlimited, boundless possibilities in one's life—a great place to welcome and express the creative urge. Occasionally, we meet in the hot tub on the point, under a starry sky or a radiant full moon, and discuss our respective projects or just marvel at the "show" the surfing dolphins provided earlier that morning. This is the California life.

It has been interesting to watch Coeleen's body of art develop over the past two years. From the initial inspiration of "The Awakening of the Feminine" to her most recent, "Brides and Black Madonnas," I have observed *her* creative process at work and learned much from it: how to make every moment count (stay active); how to bypass the creative block (plunge ahead); how to protect your private time (learn to say no to intruders); how to be disciplined (love what you're doing). It sounds easy, and Coeleen seems to glide through her life, ever elegant, even in the aftermath of a major catastrophe such as an explosion in her studio kiln.

To know Coeleen is to be struck by the similarities between her and her work. They share voluptuous female figures, often in the presence of a canine companion—a sometimes menacing, sometimes comic, always stately black giant schnauzer named Georgia.

Much of her work was destroyed in the devastating California earthquake of 1989; but, true to her nature, rather than grieving over broken pots, Coeleen proceeded to make art out of rubble. She dove back into her work with her usual diligence—this time her creative process inspired the embedding of countless shards from shattered ceramics into Miro-like whimsical mosaics on the courtyard walls surrounding her home. Her prolific outlay of work is both staggering and commendable.

Although being an artist, therapist, and teacher are full-time occupations, she still finds time for piano practice, singing in a chorus, participating in local politics, spending a significant amount of time with her partner, Ed Jackson, and, since she was diagnosed with Epstein-Barr two years ago, taking a daily afternoon nap. Full of surprises for others, I asked her when she last surprised *herself*. Coeleen laughed and declared, "I started body surfing in my fifties!"

ENOPAUSE IS DEFINITELY COMING when you cross into fifty. But whatever symptoms have presented themselves up to that point are usually called something else—you're hoping it's not menopause. There's a fear that menopause means the end of my youth, my beauty, my sexuality or vitality or energy, and it's just a matter of time until osteoporosis sets in.

Despite hearing from women on "the other side" that "it's just great," I can remember the ambivalence I had on turning fifty—that I wanted to slip into it as quietly as possible. I wasn't into having a big celebration, and I noticed that nobody else around me was into my having a big celebration—not my mate at the time or my kids. They didn't even want to recognize that I was fifty.

Any comments in my early fifties that I would make, to my children in particular, were poo-pooed. They saw me as very young, eternally young, as an exception. I think a certain part of me always did see myself as an exception to what most women my age were doing, whether I was thirty or forty. Being an exception at fifty meant that I would cruise through it, and I actually *did* cruise through menopause with very little difficulty.

I didn't toss and turn about whether to do estrogen therapy or not; I just decided to take advantage of opportunities that were there for me rather than to be swayed by the fear of what harm they might do to me. I'm very glad that I talked with my gynecologist and went along with her recommendation. I started taking estrogen—and still do—as well as the progesterone supplements for it. I'm glad I made that decision because now, ten years later, I see my contemporaries and younger women still struggling with their fears about whether or not to take hormones.

I feel that my generation has been on the cutting edge of what's happening with women. Those of us in our late fifties and early sixties were the ones who started the women's revolution, and there's never been any maps for us.

For example, the same questions that are being asked about menopause today were being asked about the Women's Movement in the '60s: "Should we or shouldn't we?" Each woman was *completely* on her own. This happened when so many women decided to try and make it independently, rather than stay in a much more comfortable and prescribed way of living.

I was the first among my circle of friends to start a consciousness-raising group. I remember when my first marriage was falling apart, I went into a bookstore to look for some literature that would help me to become a greater feminine being; feeling that if I could give my feminine nature some steroid shots, maybe my marriage would survive.

In Minnesota in 1967, they had a hard time at the local bookstore figuring out what I was looking for. And I had a hard time articulating it. They took me to the *Good Housekeeping, Ladies' Home Journal* section and pointed to Amy Vanderbilt! Then one clerk said, "Oh, there's a book that just came in which might speak to what you're asking for." She ran in the back room and came out with *The Feminine Mystique.* I told her the book looked just right, having no *idea* what I would find inside. That book absolutely changed my life.

It was springtime and I remember I called several friends and suggested that we meet at my house once a week (during the summer when we could get babysitters), just to talk about our lives. Because I couldn't handle the rejection if they said "no," I said, "Don't give me an answer now. Just think about it and come on Wednesday morning if you like." This was a totally foreign thing to do; it was coming out of my gut.

Well, the following Wednesday fifteen women arrived who brought their friends. I tried to divide the group in half, and offered Fridays as an alternative. But everybody came both days! We were all so hungry for this kind of interaction. This group lasted four years and supported me through going back to school, divorcing my husband, and then deciding to leave Minnesota and move to California with my children.

When I went back to the University of Minnesota, the Women's Reentry Program had just opened. I didn't want to sound threatening, so I assured them I was not interested in a graduate degree. Besides, I didn't think I deserved one. After about a year in school, I realized I wanted much more, and was told I could apply for graduate school only if I were willing to do something like elementary education. I wanted to study the psychology of art. My adviser told me to get serious and realize that I was the low person on the totem pole, partly because I was female and partly because of my age. Eventually, I found my way to the University of California, Santa Cruz, where I could study what I wanted.

It took me ten years to get my Master's in psychology. I was the only woman who had children in my class; it was still unusual for an older woman with children to go back to school. There *were* other women doing it, but we were so isolated from each other. I look back on those years and I just don't see how I, or the other women, survived. I was in school full time, held down a job, and raised my four kids alone. I also received some child support, and I had a $10,000 inheritance from my mother that really got me through the first three or four years. It was pretty chaotic at times. But I think it made us more authentic.

When I was in my thirties, I tried a lot of different things. Then in my forties I really rolled up my sleeves and worked very hard as an organization development consultant, and as the director of a woman's drug therapy treatment center for eight years. My art remained in the background. I had a more extroverted life as a consultant, which was probably necessary in terms of developing myself personally as well as professionally.

But when I turned fifty, I seriously began to evaluate what I wanted to do. I wondered what would happen if I took all the skills that I had developed and used them for myself as an artist instead of for outside organizations. I was willing to take the financial risk by putting my art on the front burner. My consulting continues, but it supports my art. There's also been a big shift toward teaching. I like that intimate way of being with people.

I imagine that shift is partly due to aging and the physical reality. I began to see the limited time for my career. My body cooperated with my juggling many different activities in my thirties and forties. Every once in a while it would come to a screeching halt, blasting me a message, and my back would go out for a week or even two. But I always had the energy and wherewithal to get right back in the saddle as soon as possible and continue to push. That really changed in my fifties. Now it's chronic. My body simply will no longer put up with working so hard. Whereas before I could push through for three or four weeks at a time, maybe six; now it's down to *hours*.

When I was fifty-eight, I was diagnosed with Epstein-Barr. Another aspect of feeling like I'm on the front line of women's issues in what appears to be a shocking lack of attention by professionals to women's health. It seems that the older we get, the more we are put aside. Unfortunately, through a misdiagnosis, I was treated for arthritis for eight years. I continued to be terribly fatigued and to have sore muscles. Finally, I sought the collective advice of a nutritionist, an acupuncturist, and an environmental physician. We discovered that the medication I'd been receiving for "arthritis" had depleted my system of zinc, magnesium, and calcium. That's why I'd had so much pain. Fortunately, it didn't take much to turn it around. I can't tell you how much cheaper the program I'm on now is compared with what I was doing before. I'm more relieved from the pain of arthritis since they stopped treating me for it!

Our problems are getting sloughed off as "just menopausal symptoms" or, "All women your age have those complaints." It's harder to be taken seriously by the medical profession. I feel pretty much on my own to figure out what's wrong. I'm not complaining. In fact, I think this is the new direction of medicine: that the individual has to do their own research and compile their own sources of information from the rheumatologist, the OB/Gyn, the acupuncturist and the nutritionist. I feel fortunate that I'm open to alternative medicine.

When I was in my thirties, before I moved to California, I remember making the statement that I wanted to meet an older woman who was living independently. A woman who was living a life that I would be satisfied to live. My fantasy of old age or growing older was filled with fear, because it looked pretty awful to me. My fear was that I would become stupid, inept, helpless, and living in an old people's home alone and lonely. So I wanted to find models who could give me hope. I've found wonderful models and I've continued to look for new ones.

It's more difficult for women to manifest ourselves honestly and to have what we want. There's that stress of feeling that we have to be after it and on it all the time. It's harder to earn money and to manage ourselves in the system. As a property owner, I can just see the eyes roll when I walk into a bureaucratic office. I know they would much rather deal with a man. But I enjoy my feistiness. I enjoy calling them up and telling them they can't cut down my trees in that gully to make it easier for them to work, because the animals won't have any place to live. I *know* I'm disrupting their paradigm when I say that, and I get a kick out of it!

I tell my students, "The purpose of doing art is not to become a better artist; the purpose is to become a better human being." When we become confused and get caught up in producing and marketing, our ego gets in the way. When we come into the studio with a predetermined idea about what we want to happen and start gnashing our teeth trying to make it happen, and finally become disgruntled because it doesn't "turn out right," we have missed the point. We are really in the studio to meet ourselves. That's my practice and what I try to teach people. I continually bump into myself in the studio, every day, all the time—or bump into myself, not getting into the studio.

In 1975 I made a year-long commitment to try and understand my spiritual path through my art. The first half-dozen pieces were quite disturbing. They were all female figures in a prone position, half-awake. They were like Ophelia—drifting. I realized that the first step is to realize that we are asleep. But I fought the work. I wanted to make much more heroic, Athena-like figures, but I couldn't. They were in a sleeping position and just waking up. I think that's the position we as women have a tendency to want to stay in—we want to stay asleep or go back to sleep, to be taken care of. We want to stay in this kind of balmy state of mind, and we're encouraged to stay there. So when we wake up, it's usually a crashing wake-up call through a crisis in our lives.

We'd like to have the prince come, wake us up with a kiss in a sweet, gentle way, and take us off on his horse. But it doesn't really happen that way.

When the princess wakes up, she wants to ascend immediately into an angelic state. It would be nice to just wake up and be enlightened, but first there has to be a descent—a conscious dive into the depths of her soul. There's a big difference between diving and falling. I have been thrown into the depths, and I have also chosen to take the dive. Hopefully, I don't have to crash into them anymore like I used to, which is another advantage of age. There are the times when we fall into the night terrors—those are the fears that I'm on the wrong track, or that what I've acquired will all be taken away from me, or that I will in fact grow into an old woman who is all alone and have lost my faculties. There is no angel or mascot. There's nothing there except the ghouls and gargoyles and goblins. That's what makes it authentic. The angel or mascot *might* be there, but when we're at the bottom, we don't know that.

It's at that point that the masculine comes in. We'd like it to be a man, but it has to be our own masculine energy. I have used the form of the polar bear to signify this male energy. When I was in my early fifties and going through my second divorce, I was right in that place of having to develop my own masculine energy. My fear was that I would spend the rest of my life alone. I had failed once in my first marriage, which couldn't survive my self-actualizing, and now my second marriage couldn't survive it either. The second divorce was even more devastating than the first, in part, because now I didn't have young children to divert my attention from my pain. I looked around me and saw what I had and what I didn't have, and realized I had to take responsibility for *everything* in my life: my property, my career, the quality of my life, the quality of my relationships with my children, absolutely everything. I needed all the masculine energy I could muster to make my way back up from the bottom. That's the spiritual path.

The spiritual path can be very extroverted for women. It's hard for us to recognize that our extroverted life is our spiritual path, because we've been taught to believe that our spiritual path must be introverted. Of course, it's both. After I'd done my first group of "The Awakening of the Feminine," Carol Christ's book *Diving Deep and Surfacing* was published. I saw my whole process laid out, and I realized I wasn't alone in my experience. She had articulated it in literature, and it meant a lot to me. And I could see that Betty Friedan had really started a spiritual movement. I think someday we'll recognize it as that. The Women's Movement is not just a sociological phenomena or political action. Our spiritual path is with each other, helping each other to be who we were meant to be in the world. I think we are beginning to see that the Women's Movement is one of the most important spiritual revolutions of our time.

My first marriage had to do with procreating. I had a very good partner for that. We established a nuclear family and it was appropriate for me at that time. It didn't work for me to try and make it anything else. Nor him. My second marriage had to do with putting a company together with my husband and developing myself as a consultant in the world. I learned a trade. We learned from each other, and it fulfilled itself very well in that respect; but I remember the exact day when I made the conscious decision to make art my priority.

The relationship I'm in now has got to do with companionship and mutual respect. We really do walk the same path, even though we have different professions and different interests. I met Ed, my partner, when I was in my fifties. I'd had to rewrite my life all over again after my divorce. By that time I was smart enough to ask myself, "What do I *need?*" rather than "What do I *want?*" If anything were to happen to Ed, I would feel content to be a single woman because now I have finally experienced a satisfying relationship and feel a sense of completion around that issue.

In my first marriage, I married somebody I wanted and fortunately made a good choice in terms of having my needs met for that period of my life. In my second marriage, no question about it, I married somebody I wanted. There certainly were needs of mine that got met, but they were not necessarily in my best interest. In this relationship I have been much more understanding and re-spectful of my deeper, more intelligent needs. I'm growing much more *inside* of this relationship—I sort of grew *because* of the relationships in my first two marriages. I don't regret those early relationships. There's no point in dwelling on or being angry about what happened. Time has helped me to understand the purposefulness of those relationships.

It is important to me to see what is needed and be able to fulfill those needs. I've created my life—or it's been dished out to me—and I'm responsible for it. That includes four children, a commitment with Ed, a symbiotic relationship with this land, and a way of being in the world with art. Really being able to see what is needed in all those arenas is very hard.

For example, there is something specific with each child. Now, after all the years of the Women's Liberation Movement, of wanting to be a mother and yet wanting to be liberated from my children, and trying to juggle that process so that I wouldn't be trapped (anything—cooking dinner—was a trap), I'm re-alizing that I did create this situation, I am responsible for these four children who are in their thirties. It's not like they need me to take care of them, but it's not finished. As long as I'm alive, it's not finished. So I'm responding to that fact as best I know how and acting on it.

I'm doing the best I can. I'm very pleased with what I've created, and feel a lot of gratitude about what I've been able to make of this life. The feeling of happiness is something that comes and goes when I'm with my kids or when I'm creating something in the studio. I've come to realize that the opposite of happiness is my fear and my terrors. I feel that the ultimate sin is to forget that I really am on a path, and to forget that I've been so well taken care of up to this point.

I don't think of myself as a middle-aged woman. Sometimes I think it's time I start!—although I will probably be well beyond middle-age and still not see myself as such. Often I think I should be acting differently, or feeling differ-ently, or dressing differently. When I'm shopping for clothes, I realize it would be ridiculous for me to dress in certain ways. But I just don't think of myself as being "older." I've heard people who are much older than me, whose bodies have moved further down the road of deterioration, say that they still feel very young inside. I understand what they are talking about.

I saw a video, a training tape of me that was done just about four months ago, and I was shocked that this woman on the tape was me. I just couldn't believe that I was that old. But then I dismissed that thought immediately; my defenses came right up and I went back to my inner paradigm about who I really am. My body is obviously unable to do what it was able to do five years ago, or even three. There's definitely an aging process going on. It's quite an educative process that tells me my soul and body are on two separate tracks.

This is another issue there aren't any maps for: I enjoy talking with a few other women my age who see and feel that the women who left their husbands so many years ago, like myself, did better at fulfilling their lives on their own. There's a sense of pride that comes from knowing that. One of the things these women all have in common is that the men we left said, "You'll never make it," as we walked out the door. There was a grand chorus. But we've made it. I'm proud of myself and I'm proud of them.

ISABEL ALLENDE

....

My husband and I got together very late in our lives, and we discovered a passionate love affair. There is passion for older women in mid-life. Absolutely!

profile

XXXI

A quien le puedo preguntar
que vine a hacer en este mundo?

y que me dio por transmigrar
si viven en Chile mis huesos?

Whom can I ask what I came
to make happen in this world?

and why did I decide to migrate
if my bones live in Chile?

PABLO NERUDA, *The Book of Questions*

AS I HEADED NORTH ACROSS THE GOLDEN GATE BRIDGE into Marin County, I
remembered when, three years ago, I had first invited the novelist Isabel Allende
to participate in my book, *Coming into Our Fullness: On Women Turning Forty.* To
my disappointment her reply was "no"; however, it wasn't a thoughtless or ungra-
cious refusal. Rather, within a week, I received a handwritten note on a lovely
card handmade in Chile, which showed a pastoral scene of a house with a smoking
chimney and a windmill appliqued in a variety of colorful fabrics on the front. She
had just returned from a six-month book tour promoting her latest book, *The Sto-*
ries of Eva Luna, and said she must "regretfully decline" my offer.

Considerate and prompt as usual, her response to my second request was positive. I
was elated. It wasn't until our first telephone conversation that my elation was
tempered when I learned of the personal tragedy with which she was coping. Four
months earlier her daughter, Paula, had fallen into a coma—the result of complica-
tions from the treatment of a genetic disease called porphyria. Paula, twenty-eight,
had been in Spain at the time, and recently married. Isabel had flown to Madrid to
be with her daughter, and discovered that the prognosis for recovery was not
hopeful. She decided to bring Paula back to California, where she could be kept in

Isabel's home and receive around-the-clock care from family members who had gathered there. Doctors are pessimistic about her condition. Isabel says, "I am planning my life as if there were no chance for recovery. If a miracle happens, that would be fantastic, but I'm not waiting for a miracle. I'm what you would call realistic. Or maybe older, maybe older."

We arranged to meet at Isabel's home in Marin County. The multilevel house has a sweeping panoramic view of the San Francisco Bay and the San Rafael Bridge. We spent an entire afternoon and part of a Friday evening together, and enjoyed discussing her life and work and our shared interests.

Her round, dark Latin eyes fill easily with tears, but can also reflect the joy and enthusiasm of a guileless child. Her personality and expression run the gamut from the reserved aristocracy of a queen to a passionately explicit woman to an ebulliently precocious preadolescent. Isabel literally welcomed me with open arms. As I pulled up the driveway, she was already coming down the front steps. Offering to help carry my camera equipment, she reached for my tripod, which was taller than she. Isabel is a stunning woman with dark auburn hair that frames her porcelain complexion, and an hourglass figure accentuated that day by a long print skirt in shades of brown and burgundy and worn with a wide belt. "I know what becomes me and what doesn't," Isabel said of her personal style.

Isabel has had an adventurous life. Certainly, it has been an international one. She was born in Lima, Peru, where her father, a Chilean diplomat, was then posted. After the divorce of her parents, her mother took her home to Santiago, Chile, where she formed a close relationship with her father's family while living in the home of her maternal grandparents. Life with her grandparents contributed greatly to her understanding of human beings and to her development as a writer. Isabel modeled two of the most colorful characters in her first novel, *The House of the Spirits,* after her grandparents, as well as memorializing their stately colonial home.

Following her mother's second marriage, again to a diplomat, Isabel lived with them in Bolivia and in European and Middle Eastern countries. At fifteen she returned to Chile, where she completed her education and eventually became a journalist, conducted interviews on Chilean television programs, worked on a radical feminist magazine, and wrote plays. And all this while she was raising her two children, Paula and Nicholas.

On September 11, 1973, Isabel's life was irrevocably changed when a violent military coup, headed by General Augusto Pinochet Ugarte, resulted in the death of her uncle, Salvadore Allende, who was at that time the President of Chile and the first president anywhere in the world to head a Marxist government by means of a free, multiparty election. It was also during this month that Nobel Laureate Poet Pablo Neruda, whom Isabel also knew, succumbed to cancer.

As it had been for her compatriot Neruda, for Isabel writing is both a way to ask questions and an attempt to find answers. "After my books are published," she explains, "the questions belong to other people as well. We share the questions and we all try to find the answers."

Isabel emanates a sensuousness that is *about* the senses. Much of her writing and her life is about colors and textures and sounds. Her spacious, uncluttered, well-organized home is filled with plants, colorful abstract paintings, South American *objets d'art*. Just sitting in the living room and talking with her is a sensuous experience: drinking mango tea from blue cups, which make the distinct clink of fine china when they are placed on their saucers; eating, between us, an entire package of Pepperidge Farms chocolate chip cookies, and then opening a second after Isabel notes, "I think we need more"; occasionally being startled on the half-hour by the alternate chime of a smaller clock or the gong of a larger one; basking in the lyrical quality of Isabel's voice as she sits with her knee drawn up unself-consciously and articulates a point with her hands; soaking up the splendid view of the bay with its carefree sailboats; and, not least, just *looking* at her gives one pleasure.

Isabel invited me to stay for dinner and to meet her "tribe," as she puts it. While she was downstairs caring for Paula, Willie, Isabel's husband of five years, kept me company. We discovered we had several friends in common, all of whom practice law in the Bay Area. Willie, an attorney himself, has an almost larger-than-life presence that reminded me of a character that Nick Nolte might portray: a tall, Nordic, brooding type who seems genuine about healing old wounds from an earlier, wilder time. Isabel's evident affection for her husband spills over and bathes him with the unmistakable aura of a man who is deeply loved and appreciated by a woman. To see them together is to grasp how two people can be a sort of savior for one another.

We sat down to a dinner—prepared by Isabel—of curried chicken, rice, salad, and chocolate cake with sliced strawberries. She is needlessly apologetic about her cooking skills and justifies herself by saying, "My mother cooks, maybe that's why I don't."

Her cheerful nature is a buoy in, as she says, "a tormentous sea," a decoy that tries to divert attention away from the inexpressible sorrow that visibly inhabits her soul. Her passionate nature expresses itself through the use of irrefutables—Absolutely! Certainly! Impossible! Yet, she is never overbearing, for just as easily she may temper an absolute with a maybe or a perhaps. You see the internal process right before your eyes.

Passion and love are above all else Isabel's raison d'être. Possibly, she has pursued their trail as another might follow a road map. Perhaps they are also what have comforted her in the past and continue to support her survival in the present. The original meaning of passion, after all, signified the ability to endure suffering.

VIII

Las lagrimas que no se lloran
esperan en pequenos lagos?

O seran rios invisibles
que corren hacia la tristeza?

Do tears not yet spilled
wait in small lakes?

Or are they invisible rivers
that run toward sadness?

PABLO NERUDA, *The Book of Questions*

I HAVE HAD AN ADVENTUROUS LIFE. Some parts have been very painful, other parts have been beautiful, filled with joy, a lot of love and friendship. But those painful moments were the ones when I grew the most. Looking back, I always thought those painful experiences were important in my life, and if I had to make a choice, I would go through them again. But now, with Paula's situation, it's the first time I feel totally devastated. I try to think that in a few years I will be stronger, that I will be able to look back and say, "It was good in a certain way." I don't think there is anything good about what has happened. It's a total tragedy.

When you are immersed in a situation like this, you throw overboard everything that is frivolous and superficial, because you need to be able to float. You float in tormentous waters, so you have to get rid of everything that's heavy, everything that's not meaningful or essential for survival. That's what I've been doing. When you get down to the basic aspects of your life, you realize that there *is* meaning in life, and it has to do with love.

You see, my daughter has been in a coma for a long time. Her body has changed so much that you wouldn't recognize her. Her mind is not there, yet she is there. So there is something that goes beyond the body and mind, beyond success, goals, beyond everything that we can measure. It's something that is intangible, invisible. Something like her essence is still there and I connect to that.

I sense it very much in my dreams when I'm asleep. Sometimes I will wake up suddenly and know that she is calling me. She can't talk, she has no voice right now. I run downstairs and usually there is something wrong. She can communicate better with me when I'm asleep. When I'm awake, very often I'm blocked because I'm so sad or because I'm trying to make her more comfortable or I'm dealing with all the domestic problems that one has in these circumstances. I'm so busy that I don't have time to listen to that secret voice that talks to me, and that voice is her.

So there is a meaning that goes very deeply into the soul. It's a meaning that is not only related to Paula and what has happened—*everything* has become more meaningful in my life. For example, I was planning to start a book on January 8th. On December 8th, Paula fell sick. In January, when I thought about the book, I said, "If I don't start writing, I won't be able to write at all and this year will be lost. Of course, I have not been able to write anyhow, but I thought, "I was going to write about *this?* Who cares?" The theme of the book and the writing itself became so meaningless for me because what else was going on became so *loaded* with meaning.

This experience with Paula is like exploring a land that is so full of surprises, a place where I have never been before. I have been in pain and been in difficult situations before, but I have never been in a situation in which I was *totally* out of control. I don't have control over anything. I can't even run away from it. When I was desperate in Chile during the military coup, and I was terribly afraid, I ran away with my kids. I took everybody into exile. But now I have to go through all the pain, through hell and back. It's like those great metaphors in mythology where there are heroes who go into the land of witches and dragons and devils. They have to descend into hell to rescue someone and bring that person back to the world. But in this case what I can bring back is my memory of Paula—my own perspective as a mother—because I cannot reach her.

In Latin America there are extended families with people of all ages living together in one house. My grandfather was so important in my life as I was growing up. You accept the newborn baby the same way you accept the fact that an old person becomes like a newborn baby. It's part of the chain of life. Maybe I'm not so scared of old age because I don't visualize it as being alone. At least in my family, old people are always within the family. The other day I heard on the radio something wonderful, "It takes a village to raise a child"— they were talking about Africa. It takes an extended family to raise kids, to take care of the old and the ill, to help single mothers. It takes a lot of people to *survive,* and nothing that the state can do will replace that—ever! Sure, Paula could be in a nursing home, but do you think she would be treated the way she is treated within the family? Impossible.

I don't think of myself as an individual ever. I'm part of an extended group. So whatever happens to me happens to the group. If I make a better living and more money, the whole group goes with me. And if I'm ever impoverished, I will always find refuge in that group. So, you give a lot and you receive a lot. That's the way I visualize life—as a village. It takes a village to survive.

There are two experiences that were important to me, they were painful but wonderful. The births of my kids, Paula and Nicolas, were very special moments that I'll always remember. And I remember when I saw a copy of my first book, *The House of Spirits,* in print. That's an experience that you can never repeat. You may write many books in your lifetime, but none is comparable to that first book. The thrill, the excitement, the wonder—it's fantastic.

I've learned that the only fundamental thing in life is love. You can't do anything that's really valuable without love. There are many forms of love, and all of them are important. I'm a privileged person. I first had my mother's love, which was unconditional and has been with me all these years. That was so important. It gave me a platform where I felt safe, secure, and I could do anything because my mother was there and she would protect me always. It gave me also a sense that I am lovable, so I've never doubted that. When I approach a person or when I want a man or I'm looking for a job, I never think that they won't want me. It's always a surprise when I'm rejected—I think it's only natural that people should love me, first because my mother loves me, and then because I love most people. So I resent it, I think it's terribly unfair that people should hate me, and I'm sure many people do.

I'm not currently working on anything. I don't feel like writing, and I'm just tired for right now. But I know I will go back to writing sooner or later. I will start my life again, and maybe it will be quite a different life, but I know I'm not broken emotionally. I'm devastated, but not broken. I have a strength I didn't know I had.

Willie says that I'm *too* organized, *too* punctual, *too* structured, *too* disciplined, that I'm too hard on myself. Maybe. But it works this way. I get a lot done. Willie and my kids say I should have more leisure time. I should do something for myself like go to the hairdresser or *exercise*. The latest thing is that I should see a therapist! I don't feel stressed out. There is time for each chore and then it's done, and there's something else. In that way I get through the day with no great stress. Now I have emotional stress, but usually my days are easy.

That's one of the good things about being fifty—you're not so easily scared. When I was younger, I was afraid I would not be able to earn a living and wouldn't have any money, that something might happen to my kids and I wouldn't be able to cope with it financially. I was scared that I would be alone, that no man would love me. I don't have those fears anymore.

Maybe I'm wrong, but I have the impression that when I was thirty, it was wonderful to be thirty. It was a "fad" to be thirty. Then when I was forty, everybody said, "Forty is the best time" and everyone wanted to be forty; it was splendid and glamorous and all the great actresses were forty. Now they're fifty—we're getting older. There are so many wonderful women in their fifties and they look *gorgeous*. Some are even having kids! It's a splendid time to be fifty. I suppose when I'm sixty, everybody will be thinking *that's* a great age! Of course, according to my kids, I'm ancient, totally ancient.

I haven't experienced menopause yet, but I'm sure it will be like menstruation was for me—something will just happen to my body and I won't even think about it. I've never thought much about menopause. Someone once said that you have the menopause you deserve! So I think if I don't worry too much about it, maybe it will happen very easily.

At fifty I feel physically strong. I don't exercise, I don't diet, I don't take pills of any kind, I don't care about my body—I don't even think about it. I can endure a lot. I can be overworked and underslept for weeks and still go on. My body is still very resilient, although I'm aware that there's a point at which it will say, "Enough is enough. I've done enough for you," and it will just fall apart. It *will* happen eventually, and at that point, I'll have to reconsider the way I live. Right now I just demand of my body everything I need. I sleep a little and work a lot. I never think about having a backache if I lift something heavy, or if I eat fat that it's bad for my cholesterol. I haven't seen my cholesterol, so I don't care. It's like bacteria—I've never seen bacteria, so I don't believe in it. They were invented by doctors.

I hate exercise. I hate to sweat when I don't have to, to run to a place when I don't have to get there at all—if you're not late, why would you? Or to get in a swimming pool and get your hair wet—I think that's awful. But everyone says it's good for you, so maybe it's true, maybe it *is* good for you. The same thing with dieting: why diet and exercise so much? By the time we are seventy, my friends who exercise will look just as bad as I will. Why would they go all through this trouble when you can hide everything with the right clothes?

After fifty most of the bullshit is gone. I don't have any time to waste. I don't have time for gossip or greed or revenge or undirected anger. I'm angry at very concrete things now and focus it into action. I know myself much better. I know my body and I know what becomes me and what doesn't. I don't make the mistake of wearing miniskirts, for example. I look terrible in pants and miniskirts. I know how to dress so that I feel more confident than I *ever* did before. I don't want to look younger, and I'm not interested in being attractive to men in general. I want to be sexually attractive to Willie—not always—at certain, very specific moments, because I'm not interested in being sexually attractive all the time.

I'm not jealous at all because I feel that if my husband is so stupid that he would chase another woman, he might just as well go, leave, because I'm not going to bother fighting for him. I have a life and wonderful relationships I'm comfortable with. I'm positive I will always have another man in my life. I'm absolutely sure I will have sex until I'm eighty if I want to.

I've always felt that way about men. The difference is that now I don't care if I am with a man or not. If I'm alone, I'm okay. I don't need to be with a man to be well. Now that I am with Willie, I feel great, but if he goes, I won't be placing ads in newspapers or going to a dating service. I'm not interested. I *love* my job, I love to write. It gives sense to my life. For eight or ten hours a day, I am in another world. It's fantastic! This is the first time in my life I can really do what I like on my terms—it's a great moment in my life.

So I'm enjoying everything that I can do now and also look forward to the next stage. My mother is seventy. She's always been twenty years ahead of me. Now I look at her and see what I'm going to be at seventy. My mother is a *fabulous* human being—I say, "If she can do it, so can I. If she can be so curious, so naive and innocent, always ready to accept things, to investigate and explore new territories, then it's wonderful." You can be seventy and still be young. I see a good future for myself. When I was forty, I thought being fifty was the end of the road and I'd have to commit suicide because I'd have wrinkles and white hair; now I'm looking forward to all that. I don't resent it.

Although, I would have plastic surgery if that was important for me. It's something I'm open to. I think if there's a point when I look at myself in the mirror and I dislike something that is sagging—I don't mind wrinkles, but I don't like things hanging down—and it could be eliminated in forty-five minutes in an operating room, I'd do it. Of course. I wouldn't consider having breast implants because I'm too old for that. I would have done it when I was thirty maybe, but now, why would I?

My husband and I got together very late in our lives, and we discovered a passionate love affair. There *is* passion for older women in mid-life. Absolutely! I'm madly in love with this man, and I think that he's gorgeous. There is love at any age, a lot of it. By the time we met, my children were already grown, but we were dealing with Willie's kids and his business. Finally, in November 1991, everything was clear in our lives: his office was working fine, his children were in school, and we were at last alone in this house. Everything was organized and neat. We had a great housekeeper who kept everything perfect. It lasted for about fifteen days. So here we are now, living all together with my children and their partners and my grandchildren—everybody is here. We are like a tribe. In a way, that part is good; I like the family being close. And Willie is accepting it quite well. He is surviving also.

I think that my natural vocation is marriage. I like to be with one person, to share secrets with him; I like to sleep in the same bed with the man I love. There is a lot in marriage that I like very much. There is a complicity that is established without words. It comes out of having sex and sleeping in the same bed and sharing a toothbrush with the same person on a daily basis.

I come from a family of very strong women. In Chile, and in most of Latin America, the women are strong. In order to survive in a patriarchal society, you have to be organized, you have to have good women friends. There is a network of female friends who survive in this patriarchal culture. They survive in spite of men. Women have very rough lives. I've worked with women and for women all my life, and I know that they have most of the responsibilities and very few rights or privileges. They are usually the ones who are in charge of the family and left alone with the kids without support from the father. Women do double the work and get half the recognition of any man in any job. They are usually much stronger and *much* more interesting human beings. Men are more interesting to me in bed, but for the rest of everyday life, women are more interesting in every sense. I seldom find myself talking about really important matters with men, but I can immediately communicate deeply with women.

Women are more process oriented than goal oriented. Very seldom does the end justify the means for a women. I think this has to do with the fact that women are biologically inclined to raise children. Raising children is not a goal, it's a process—something that you do constantly, like a journey—it never ends. There is no recognition; there is no goal, it's just being.

The first time I could articulate a feminist thought was after reading Germaine Greer's *The Female Eunuch* when I was twenty-six. That was the first time I realized there was a language for feminism. Before that I was a feminist and I was writing a feminist column, but I didn't call it feminism. I wrote a humorous column in which I made fun of men and denounced the macho ways in our culture. Men loved it and thought it was very funny. They all thought they had a friend who was very much like the character in my column—it was always a friend, never themselves.

So when feminism really started in Chile, I was automatically called "the first feminist." But the truth is I had no idea what I was writing about. Later, I worked on a feminist magazine with a team of feminist women. They were professional journalists—I was a housewife who was writing stories in the dining room. They taught me a lot.

I'm a fiction writer, and by telling stories, I try to find a meaning to my own life and for things that happen in real life. I'm not a very analytical person. That's why I've never been in therapy, because I think it would be extremely boring to be telling someone your problems over and over. I'd rather write a story, and through the story I find a little clue to something that is important to me. I ask myself always, "Why am I writing this? Why is it so important to me?" It's usually because I'm looking for something that is useful in my real life. After the book is written, I discover I've been writing about myself all the time.

When I wrote *Eva Luna,* for example, it had nothing to do with me or my life. The character was a mixture of races from the Caribbean part of the continent, she was a poor, marginal woman who was illiterate and brought up in the streets. I come from a totally different situation, a very protected environment. I thought the book had *nothing* to do with me. And then, later, I began receiving papers written by students and professors, in which they compare me with Eva Luna. At first I thought those guys were crazy; then when I read what they had written, I realized there was a lot of truth in what they were saying. I'd been writing about being a woman and the struggle for a woman to be herself in a patriarchal society; about being marginal and not belonging anywhere; about being a storyteller and the importance of stories; and about what language can do for your life—when you can articulate something, it then becomes part of your reality; before you articulate it, it's just confusion.

The difference between me and many women writers in Latin America is that I was not first published in Latin America—I was published in Europe, and that's why my work was reviewed, studied, and translated. Women have been writing in Latin America for centuries; we have had great writers of fiction and nonfiction, and great poets. They were ignored, silenced. There is a sort of conspiracy of silence among professors, reviewers and the press in South America; they have systematically ignored the work of women. So it's not as if I'm the only woman writer; it's that I was very lucky that my book was rejected everywhere in Latin America. Maybe the fact that I was successful in Europe and America opened a door for other writers who had not been published before.

The success of my books has changed my life dramatically. I can support myself, to begin with. I can choose where to live and what to write about. I don't have a boss or have to spend eight hours a day in a job. I do as I please, and I can help my family and other people the way I like. I'm totally independent. Before my first book was published, I felt isolated, almost paralyzed. Now I have the feeling that I'm in action, more a part of the world. I know what's going on and I can express my ideals.

It would not be true if I said that success hasn't been important. If my first book had not been published, I wouldn't have written the second one. My personality is not such that I will continue on with something that is not working. I am driven to write, but I chose to write fiction late in my life. I was thirty-nine when I wrote *The House of the Spirits,* and I had never written fiction before. I had been a journalist and I loved to write, so I would have gone back to journalism. It's not that I decided to be a novelist; it just happened and I was successful. It was as if a road was opened to me that I had not thought about taking before.

When I'm writing I lock myself in my room. There are lots of demands that I can't control. People ask me to do all sorts of fund raising and interviews, students who are writing papers want me to edit them, teachers who are using my books in their classes want me to come and talk to the students. There are many demands in the mail. I really need time to concentrate. If I decide to go back to writing, which I will probably do next year, I need to lock myself in my room—absolutely! By then, I should have everything running in this house. I'm sure it will happen.

I don't believe there is a god—not the God we were taught, not a person I can relate to, whom I can ask things from, whom I can pray to, or who cares if I do right or wrong and will punish or reward me. But I believe there is a spirit and there is something wonderful called the Creation, which works like a perfect pattern. There is a sort of synchronicity in everything. Everything is interrelated. So I'm part of that design—my soul and my spirit are part of it. I have a role here, a place, a color, a tone. If I do wrong, it affects the whole pattern. If I do right, it does as well. There are choices all the time and you make the right choices because it's convenient, not because you are going to be punished or rewarded.

What triggered *Plan Infinito* was my love for Willie and the fascination I have for this kind of self-made person. He's a real marginal, I love that about him. I come from a society in Chile that is like a cake of many layers. The social classes are like castes in India—you belong there and are forever stuck. I was able to get away from that because I left the country. I was pushed out. That's why I have been able to make a life in spite of my background. So I'm always fascinated with people who don't have this rigid set of rules, and don't have to comply with other people's traditions or history.

When I begin a book, I usually feel there is something growing in the womb, not in the mind. Then I sit down on January 8th with a little ceremony that I have, and write the first sentence. Usually, I don't know where that first sentence leads, or what will come next, but it's like opening a door and you enter into an unknown place and things begin to unfold as you give them time. I need time alone in silence in a quiet place every day from eight to four, let's say, more or less, without interruptions, without the telephone, without coffee breaks, without lunch. And that time is sometimes spent doing nothing. Perhaps reading or researching, but mostly, writing things that I won't use. I'm getting in the mood of the book. It's a very tedious process. I know that most writers form an outline and follow chapters, they are more organized and have people who research for them. I'm messy. I just sit down and pour everything out. Out of that *huge* amount of writing—which is usually about a thousand pages—I put together the novel.

I tell people, "If you want to write, write! Don't study. Don't try to copy anybody else, just write. And by doing it, you'll get there if you have a vocation." People think that writing is sitting down and writing a book that will be famous immediately. Most of the time writing is just hard work with no recompense. So if you are able to get through that long period during which you are starving and you aren't published or even receiving any feedback, then you really have a vocation; you really want to write, so do it. When you are beginning to write, it is important to keep a distance from the characters: don't write in the first person, don't be you, don't try to tell the truth. Writing is lying. Once you accept that it's a lie, from the very beginning, then you feel free to write anything. You don't have to explain, just go ahead and write.

As far as my politics is concerned, my uncle, Salvadore Allende, didn't have a big influence on me. Of course, in 1970, when his government won the election, there was a coalition of parties from the left and the center. The Socialist Party was just one of the many parties of the coalition. I wasn't very clear about politics at that time. I didn't care. But during Allende's government, the country was divided into two opposing factions, and it was impossible to remain neutral. You had to take up arms, I would say, because the country was so divided. I mean sides, but I call it arms because it was a real war. Not that we had a gun at home, but it was a fight, a struggle. It was like a war zone.

I remember that my in-laws were very much against Allende, and our relationship became very difficult because politics interfered in everything. You couldn't have dinner with your own in-laws without getting into a fight. The neighborhoods were divided; it was awful. At that time, I think that because I had been so aware when I was little of the differences between the rich and the poor in my country, about how few opportunities the people had, and how the rich groups had *all* the privileges, that it was natural that I would go with the left and with Allende.

The three years of Allende's presidency were an extraordinary time in Chile. It was a very difficult time also. You couldn't get anything because everything was rationed and you couldn't buy anything—money was worth nothing. However, things happened in the streets. People were empowered. New songs and new art flourished. There was something happening that was so explosive, so full of life, so full of hope. People who had never had anything said they were rich for the first time because they had an opinion, they had a government that represented them. I was fascinated by that process and very shocked when the military coup overthrew Allende. It ended one hundred years of democracy in that country. I remember that day as one of the worst days in my life. Everything changed in twenty-four hours.

I stayed in Chile thinking that democracy would return. As I became more and more involved in helping people and hiding them, there came a point when I had to leave. I felt so threatened; I was so scared. I left first, and a month later my husband sent the kids, and then he left. At first, when I couldn't go back to Chile, I longed for it desperately. Then I married Willie and came to live in California. Even though I don't belong here, I feel at home. I don't speak very well the language and I feel a total foreigner, but in a strange way, it's home. Now I love going back to Chile and I always say, "I would love to come back and stay and end my life in Chile." But who knows what will happen in the future?

SUMAHSIL

We have to remember how valuable we are as resources and appreciate and respect that fact. The gifts we have at fifty sure don't have a lot to do with what our bodies look like. In our society "elder" and "older" have been maligned, so it's important to say with joyous dignity, "I am an elder."

profile

Though there is no public rite of passage for the woman approaching the end of her re-
productive years, there is evidence that women devise their own private ways of marking
the irrevocability of the change. Menopause is a time of taking stock, of spiritual as well
as physical change, and it would be a pity to be unconscious of it.

GERMAINE GREER, *The Change: Women, Aging and the Menopause*

IN AUGUST 1992 I WAS INVITED TO SPEAK at a full moon gathering of women.
It would be a rite of passage, a ceremony, I was told, for Women of the Fourteenth Moon—menopausal women—and an opportunity for women of all ages
(maiden, mother, or crone) to reclaim aspects of ourselves. Would I speak on what
it means to me to be a mother, to be a woman in her forties—not yet
menopausal—still experiencing and loving her bleeding-time? The whole point of
doing service through ceremony is to be able to say yes. I said, "Yes!"

Awaiting me atop Dharma Ridge in the California mountains above Santa Cruz
was an extravagant and delicious assortment of nearly one hundred glorious
women, a composite of the Rainbow Coalition. Their beauty was not determined
by or limited to a specific age, size, body shape, race, sexual preference, or socioe-
conomic background. The diversity of femaleness itself was a feast for the senses.
We had been asked to dress in a manner "reflecting the spirit of woman—graceful,
comfortable, and festive"; we did. Long, fluttering, colorful skirts; embroidered
ethnic vests; glittering beaded jewelry dangling from earlobes, wrists, necks, ankles,
and waists; loose hair tossing like a salad in the sunlight; bodies prancing like wild
ponies ornamented the mountaintop. Wild women: free, uninhibited, liberated,
unbridled, at once sensuous and sensual.

As women have been doing for millennia, we sang, we told stories, we *listened* to
stories, we ate, we howled at the moon, we danced for ourselves, we danced for
each other, we hugged, we praised the Earth, we tended the fire, we celebrated
our womanhood and one another. We were perfectly aware that it is through our
senses we stay juicy and connected to the Cosmic Juice, and that this is a time for
us as women to revel in our sensuousness with a serious abandon. We were reminded that in order to save or regain our sanity, we must cultivate a basic and
primary relationship to plants and animals and the natural world. For it is through
doing this that we feel a sense of well-being in our bodies and in our souls.

The woman responsible for this annual gathering of the family of women—Women of the Fourteenth Moon—is Eleanor Piazza, also known as Sumahsil. Her dream is that "on every full moon, somewhere, there will be women of all ages and backgrounds gathering to celebrate and honor the strong, wise, compassionate and gloriously unique old woman who dwells within each of us." Sumahsil coined the term "Women of the Fourteenth Moon" as an honoring name for menopausal women. "Simply," she explains, "if there are thirteen full moons in a given year, a woman who has not had a period for a year will begin a new phase in her life upon the fourteenth full moon without bleeding. For most women, unless they have had a hysterectomy, there are skips and starts, so it can take a long time to achieve this status. It is cause for celebration." She feels that having moon in the name is important because it identifies women with the cycles of nature.

Menopause marks the beginning of "the little-mapped passage of postreproductive life," writes Gail Sheehy in *The Silent Passage: Menopause.* "Until quite recently it was rarely talked about—even among women." During the next two decades, an unprecedented 40 to 50 million women will undergo menopause. Women will not only begin talking about their menopause, but will write (and are writing) about their experiences: physical, emotional, and spiritual.

What began as a desire by Sumahsil to provide a celebration to a personal friend who had passed a full year without a period has now become a seven-year tradition of women renewing their solidarity with women as well as a vision with international proportions: in 1994 the conch—symbol of the awakening of the Feminine—will be carried to Italy, where a ceremony will be organized.

To quote Germaine Greer: "Nowadays, the whole idea of age is considered obscene. We are not allowed to call ourselves old; still less is anyone else allowed to call us old. We are now supposed to stay young and both sexually attractive and sexually active until the utterly unmentionable end, death." If Sumahsil has anything to say about it, women will learn to joyously embrace their "elderhood."

She is a woman with a *force tranquille,* a gentle strength. Her round form exudes a combination of nurturance and sexuality. There is a comforting kind of homespun wisdom in her words—in *what* she says as well as *how* she says it. You know you are listening to a woman who is not just spewing forth theory, but bounteously sharing her life experiences. Sumahsil seems like the kind of best friend of whom everybody dreams: someone who will listen to your troubles and offer solace, feed you a restorative bowl of chicken noodle soup, and tenderly tuck you into bed. You know when you wake up things will be better—because they already are. This is the ambiance Sumahsil provides in her Women of the Fourteenth Moon circles. It starts with her and radiates outward.

I CALL MYSELF A CEREMONIALIST. I use the heightened moments, the purposefulness, the concentration and focus of ritual to realign myself with the spirit of woman. For me, ceremony contains the excitement and wonder of an archaeological dig, only instead of finding remnants of an ancient civilization, I touch in with the soul of a culture gone by. My preliterate self embraces the side of me that knows about computers, and I find a sense of wholeness in this.

This week the health editor of "CNN News" is filming a segment of my ceremony, Women of the Fourteenth Moon, to include in a series on menopause. I told her we would use CNN as an electronic conch shell to get the word out to women everywhere that menopause and mid-life are cause for celebration. I like the balance that can be struck between ancient visions and technological efficiency.

In my teens and twenties, fresh off the farm in Templeton, California, I was an adventurer. With the hounds of mediocrity nipping at my heels, I hitch-hiked all over Europe for a year or so, studying in Paris and working in the south of France. I married when I returned, and—typical of the '60s woman—helped put my husband through law school, while I got my Master's Degree in French at San Francisco State. I studied in the day and waitressed at the Top of the Mark Hopkins and the Hotel Fairmont on Nob Hill until two in the morning. Unfortunately, the occupational hazard of this work can be alcoholism, and I struggled with this for a long time.

My thirties were filled with drama! I felt suffocated in my marriage, and after nine years struck out on my own again. I didn't know I was part of a wave of women who were fighting for autonomy of the psyche. We didn't really have any models or mentors to guide us through these times. I felt so bad about leaving my husband that I signed quit claim deeds to the properties we owned together, in order to assuage my guilt. I later regretted that action and suffered its consequences, as many women have done.

I became very politically active, and survived by generating some money with a weekly column, some freelance articles, and, for a while, food stamps. I was also writing and publishing poetry and involved with organizing the Santa Cruz Poetry Festivals. I fought like mad to get a few women poets and writers represented at these events. At one festival I helped organize, where Charles Bukowski and Lawrence Ferlingehtti were reading, I came on stage supposedly to read a poem, but instead I read a statement condemning the sexist policies of the male organizers and I tore the festival poster in half as a protest. The women in the audience cheered my action.

In my late thirties, I was working as a paralegal helping women, primarily, to get out of their marriages with more of their rights intact than I had when I left. I stopped abusing alcohol; and, after releasing my drinking ritual, I felt bereft for a while, because I had nothing to replace it with. That was when I was led to a Native American spiritual community, where I lived and worked for three years and where I really defined my life. I pretty much jumped off the planet for those years—goodbye electricity, traffic, telephones, and television. I got off the fast track and found a form for my spirituality.

After I left the community, I was missing ceremony in my life because I had been steeped in the Native American experience. I didn't know how to rein-state it. On the full moon, I would have a few women over to do ritual, but I was not willing to be a leader. I didn't want to be a "wannabe"—I wanted to perform ceremony from my place as a white woman and not imitate what I saw others doing. It took a long time to be able to assimilate all that I had learned and let the event itself speak to me, teach me. I learn from the cere-mony. It is an entity unto itself, and it teaches me about power and control, about giving and receiving, about humility, self-esteem, appreciation, friend-ship, community, and much, much more.

There is a real hunger for ceremony; women really want it. Since our Women of the Fourteenth Moon ceremony can't accommodate everybody, it is my dream that women who attend will take this idea and go back to their own communities and find their poets, playwrights, singers, dancers, and fire keepers and offer their own ceremony. Even if there are only four or five of them gathering together—in the name of femininity, in the name of Woman Spirit, in the name of their wisdom—in their backyards, on their decks or in their living rooms. We must create ceremonies appropriate for our own com-munities.

We are going through a big revision in religion and spirituality at this time in history. There are the women who want to become rabbis in the synagogue or priests in the Catholic church; there are pagans and neopagans. I just try to fill a need in my own heart, a need for living ceremony, which is different from ritual. Ritual is the same thing over and over. I like the fact that cere-mony is always changing. I like the spontaneous things that occur and how they get incorporated into the next year's ceremony. It's important that there's no stagnation.

So much healing can occur in women's lives right now if women will use the aspects of ceremony to go within themselves, and I think more and more women are. I notice that instead of wedding showers and bachelor parties, where people go out and get drunk, I'm asked to do more "blessing ways"— ceremonies in which people come together to bless and honor the way of their friends. I am a Universal Life minister and have been conducting wedding ceremonies for fifteen years. I notice that people are becoming much more interested in the content of their vows. They are more poetic and sincerely concerned with how they spend their lives together. So the essence of the ceremony is coming back around, I think, because it has become so empty.

Creating a ceremony is a way of putting the sacred back into life. Birthdays and anniversaries are rites of passage and opportunities to see what we have accomplished during the past year. A child has many opportunities for honoring rites of passage: their birth and successive birthdays, graduation from grammar school and high school, the onset of menses. Every day we can honor someone we know or an action like drilling a well or building a house or greeting the sun. Sometimes we observe these passages, but they seem to have become habits now.

Ceremony also affects my personal life with my husband. I am fifty-two and my husband is eleven years younger than me. I have never had children, so I don't have that gauge, which many women have, of seeing their children graduating from college or giving birth to their own children. It's always a shock when I look in the mirror and think, "Who is that person?" because I forget how old I am on the outside when I feel so young in my heart.

Four years ago I had a hysterectomy; they thought I had ovarian cancer because the sonogram showed some big black blobs. When I came out of the anesthesia, my husband had his hands through the bars on the side of the bed and was looking me in the eyes and he said, "You and me, babe, you and me." It blew me away.

Six months to a year after the surgery, my sexual desire was zip, room temperature, and that was very hard on him. He let me know the whole time that this was not working for him, that it was not okay. I was experiencing a form of depression, or what I call "when the lights go out and the music stops." You can't separate spirit and sexuality, so I won't say it was just sexuality—it was everything. I was taking a very low dosage of estrogen at the time. I went to my nurse practitioner and we slightly increased the amount of estrogen I was taking. It was amazing: the lights went back on and the music started playing again! I, too, would have been enraged had I been a younger woman with an older man who said, "Sorry, honey, I can't get it up anymore." I would have said, "What do you mean? Do you want me to just die sexually?"

Many women think it's unnatural to take hormone replacement therapy and that they shouldn't do it, they should only take natural herbs. I think it's wonderful to take Chinese herbs; I also experimented with all of that before I had my hysterectomy. But it's important to remember that at the turn of the century, natural was *death*. We didn't live beyond our parts. We didn't have opportunities to have hysterectomies; if we got ovarian cancer, we died. I'm alive and I want to stay that way. I want to keep myself lubricated, and if that means taking estrogen, I'll do it. As one doctor put it: "When a woman has had both her ovaries and her uterus removed, it would be criminal to not recommend estrogen replacement therapy."

It was vital for me to experiment with estrogen, and it's important for women not to be hard on themselves if they're depressed due to a loss of estrogen. It can't always be taken care of with a pill or a patch, however—it's not that simple—we still have to eat right and exercise properly. If our ovaries don't give us estrogen, our adrenals are important in moving estrogen through the system. I have extra padding and store estrogen in my fat, but thin women don't even have that. It was scary thinking that my sexuality might never return to me, but I looked around and noticed that my creativity was on a down slide and my spirit was at low ebb. Estrogen replacement therapy is about more than just reducing hot flashes.

I think there's always some kind of intimacy and companionship with women that can *never* be substituted or replaced by a man. It's just very different. I can't believe all the things I want to do now that I'm in my fifties. I've just taken belly dancing classes, a watercolor class, a doll-making class; I give workshops, I work and I write. I don't have enough time in a day to do all I want to do. This is an exciting time in my life. The days seem to be getting shorter. I was talking about this with a friend, and she said, "Our only enemy right now is time." It feels like this is so.

I am writing a book based on my ceremony, Women of the Fourteenth Moon, called *Wise Women, Holy Women: Rites of Passage to Elderhood*. The book is about fifty- and sixty-year-old women saying, "I am an elder" and feeling good about it. In our society, "elder" and "older" have been maligned, so it's important to say with joyous dignity, "*I* am an elder." I just want to stay with the sweetness of that knowing. I think my book is timely: it gives dignity and self-esteem to the whole wave of baby-boomers who are transforming themselves into elders with consciousness.

Now that I'm in my fifties, I'm looking at menopause and doing ceremonies and celebrations for other women in their fifties; I'm sure when I'm in my sixties, I'll be working with other aspects of aging. I just want to make whatever stage I'm in my project.

Ceremony is such a gift. I come in contact with such glorious women. I'm in heaven. I created that for myself. I know I'll continue to create beautiful things. I don't know what I'll be stepping into next, but I hope it sponsors me because it's very hard to sell oneself to another person. It's almost degrading when you know so much and have so many talents and skills. My task now is to create my own job.

With few exceptions, working has always been something I did to "pay the rent." I've worked in crazy, awful receptionist jobs in between teaching and writing. I never paid much attention to a job or took them too seriously. It's been a blessing because I never got head-over-heals into some profession that I couldn't back out of gracefully—I was ready to hitchhike off at the drop of a hat. It's been a blessing, but, in another way, it's been difficult not to have some kind of regularity. I need to make my own way, to support myself. I can't ask somebody else to do that.

The tool of ceremony is helping me become more quiet and centered, deeper and more useful, more playful. If I can give that gift to others, what more could I ask for? Ceremony affects the individual, the individual affects the family unit, the family unit affects the community circle and the community circle affects global relationships. I think it radiates out.

My vision is that every woman will have the opportunity to experience standing in a full moon circle sometime in her life and honoring herself as a maiden, matron or elder. American society has been youth-worshiping; I had to go to another culture to find out the beauty of elderhood. There's only one way to go—everybody's going to be elders pretty soon; the majority are heading toward it. We have to *know* we're beautiful. It would be an awful world to live in with people who didn't like themselves and didn't appreciate their elderhood. That's my quest, to say how rich elderhood can be for women.

Then the next step, I suppose, will be on death and dying, and the beauty of that transition. I can see that just as I'm passing gracefully into old age, I will pass gracefully into that next transition into death, because I will have researched it, done ceremonies about it. I'm sure I will talk to people who are dying, hold hands with the dying, laugh and cry with them, just as I'm holding hands with the aging and honoring them. I think the only way is to plunge headlong into each new phase.

When I was thirty-two years old, I was in my first women's group. We sat in a circle and the facilitator had each one of us tell something we would like to be different about our bodies. There were these gorgeous women saying, "I wish my collarbone didn't stick out." By the time we went around the circle, we all got it—that everyone sees flaws in their bodies and is dissatisfied with how they look. I've learned to have more respect for my body than I did when I was a fashion plate, and to give thanks for my good health.

Sometimes I help out at a friend's store that sells resort clothes and bikinis. Generally, the women come in and say, "Oh, no, I couldn't wear that—I've gained a pound" or an ounce or whatever. The most beautiful thing happened one day: A beautiful, beautiful blond woman came into the store. Even though she was in a wheelchair, she chose several bikinis that suited her hair and coloring and what-not, and wheeled herself to the dressing room. She had no use of her body from the waist down and she simply asked me if I would remove the chair after she'd lifted herself out with her hands. Afterwards, she made a selection and was happy and lighthearted. Not once did I hear her remark about her body size or shape. She seemed so grateful, so thrilled to have use of her torso, her arms, and that she would be sitting in the sunshine and tanning. It so highlighted the attitude of most of the other women who came into the store.

There needs to be much discussion about our bodies. There is a full-figured, beautiful goddess being presented to us in a lot of ceremonies and women's art. That's important. For my European ancestors just one hundred years ago, the models of Manet and Renoir were full-bodied women. We've got this disease in our society with anorexia and trying to please the patriarchy.

We spend so much time in denial and not accepting our bodies or fighting weight—I know I have. Having a man who thinks I'm beautiful is lovely, but first of all we must say to ourselves we are beautiful—and believe it. If I hadn't thought I was beautiful, I probably wouldn't have had the courage to be with a man who is younger than me. We have to make a new vision of what a beautiful woman is—each of us. We have to spend time appreciating ourselves.

Another factor concerning women in their middle years is their appreciation of their minds. Whenever I have the opportunity to talk to women, I encourage them to go back to school (if they haven't already)—take a class at a local junior college just to see how wise they already are. A woman in her forties or fifties can go into a reentry program and think, "I've lost it; I don't have any skills." But when she goes into the classroom, she finds that she is often head and shoulders above the younger students. She can read circles around these kids, and has so much of her own worldly knowledge to bring to her term papers. It really enhances her self-esteem to know how wise she already is.

We have a solidness about us, a kindliness, a laser-beam clarity. We see the big picture. We can help our younger sisters who are struggling with something that is important to them. We can hug 'em and let 'em cry, or just be quiet in their presence—sometimes that's all we need to do. We have to remember how valuable we are as resources and appreciate and respect that fact. The gifts we have at fifty, sixty or seventy sure don't have a lot to do with what our bodies look like. As elders we have so much to give.

TABRA TUNOA

Now that I'm almost fifty, I'm discovering that maybe I don't have to have a man, and also that I don't have to be that beautiful because my women friends like me fine just the way I am.

profile

A PASSION FOR THE EXOTIC AND THE COLORFUL IN TRAVEL, cultures, clothes, jewelry, art, and men has been a consistent quality in Tabra Tunoa's character. She grew up in the rather prosaic midwestern states of Oklahoma, Kansas, Arkansas, Nebraska, and Texas, where her parents' occupation as professors of American Literature took the family to a variety of Christian colleges. Tabra remains grateful to her parents for instilling in her a love of reading about different cultures, but her greatest influence was *National Geographic*.

When she was fourteen, Tabra fell in love with a man from Samoa who was taking a class with each of her parents at a small college in Nebraska. When she was eighteen, they eloped and went to live in Samoa; there, her son, Tangi, was born. The young family stayed together for four or five years until "irreconcilable differences" brought Tabra back to Texas, where, as a single mother, she began to raise Tangi. It was a prejudiced environment for a child who was half-Samoan, and Tabra began to develop a defiant insistence on justice and equality for all peoples.

Living in Samoa had sparked her childhood fantasies of traveling and living in foreign lands. With a degree in art and a master's in English, Tabra was qualified to teach. So for several years, she and Tangi traveled to and lived in the Samoan Islands, Costa Rica, Spain, the Virgin Islands, Mexico City, New York, and the Mexican border of Texas, where she taught English as a second language to migrant workers.

In the early '70s, California called. Tabra and her son moved to Berkeley, which welcomed ethnic diversity and individuality. A night class in jewelry making in Barcelona had been the impetus for Tabra to begin making jewelry; Telegraph Avenue in Berkeley proved to be the ideal place to sell it. "I saw Telegraph Avenue and I loved it. It was just what I wanted. It was like a foreign country." Tabra threw off her strict Church of Christ upbringing and "just dropped out. I didn't pay taxes, I didn't own a car, I didn't own anything. I started selling my jewelry on the street, which upset my parents because they felt that all my education was for nothing. They were afraid I was going to be a 'carnie.'"

She remembers wheeling her jewelry up the street in a shopping cart and living "like a gypsy"—traveling around the world for supplies and selling what she made.

"I was living such an unorganized, wild life." But her Telegraph Avenue days are long gone. Tabra's business (called "Tabra") has become a nearly $5 million-a-year corporation that was noted in *Inc. 500*—the magazine of the top five hundred fastest-growing small businesses in the United States—two years in a row.

Raising her son as a single woman proved a difficult task. "When my son turned fifteen, he wouldn't go traveling with me anymore. He became a real problem because he was totally out of control. I never had a man to help me and he got so big, so fast. I wasn't good at disciplining him, giving him limits or being consistent. The only men I brought home were total disasters, so Tangi didn't have good male role models. The men I've been involved with were often drug addicts, alcoholics, physically abusive to me and even drug dealers."

Seven years ago, Tabra disengaged from these destructive liaisons and her business took off—it doubled every year for three years. Even during the recession, it has held its own. Walking into the huge beige and evergreen warehouse in the town of Novato in northern Marin County, I was intrigued by the mini–United Nations feel to the spacious workroom. Close to a dozen international flags are draped from an upper balcony for all to see. Flags from Laos, Vietnam, Cambodia, El Salvador, Mexico, Ethiopia, China, Taiwan, and America. Out of seventy-five workers in Tabra's operation, about sixty-five of them are refugees, and each ethnic group is represented by its own flag. Whenever they hire a person from a new country, the organization is thrilled because "we get to put up a new flag."

It is Tabra's vision to bring together "people from all over the world, including homosexuals, lesbians, people with disabilities, old and young people alike, who can work together and get along." Anyone who can't "get along" is promptly fired. One man was fired because he sexually harassed some of the Asian women; another was fired because he refused to take orders from a woman who was his supervisor; and several have been fired because of racial discrimination among the workers.

To her credit, Tabra has several reasons for being in business: beyond the obvious motives of earning a living doing something she loves, which is making art jewelry, her altruistic motive is not just to make money but to change the world in some way. This year the corporation joined Social Venture Network (other participants are Anita Reddick's The Body Shop and Ben and Jerry's Ice Cream), an organization of companies that are making $5 million a year or more and are interested in taking their business in a socially responsible direction.

Tabra is her own best advertisement for her dazzling earrings, bracelets, and belts. The afternoon we met she was bejeweled in a plethora of jangling silver bracelets and a vest made from handwoven Bolivian wool that she had decorated with so many handmade copper discs that whenever she moved she sounded like a carefree wind chime. After a tour of the warehouse and a demonstration of how the ear-rings are handmade, polished, and buffed, Tabra invited me to visit her home, which is about a twenty-minute ride from the warehouse if you're driving with Tabra in her speedy Saab. Situated in a glen of oak trees near George Lucas's compound in Marin County north of San Francisco is the rambling wood-paneled house that Tabra calls home. It is filled with the treasures of her decades of travel. She guided me on a tour and pointed out each Mola from San Blas, each rug from Turkey, the matching set of a pair of many-colored leather sandals and shoulder bag from Indonesia, the antique coral-colored glass bead necklace that was worn by concubines in the Nagaland region in India, the mudcloth textiles from Africa—two floors and many rooms worth of hand-selected prizes—as if she were introducing me to a group of her most appreciated friends.

Tabra's plans for travel and adventure remain undiminished, "If I'm going to be an artist, I have to go to these fascinating countries, even to the difficult ones like India and Africa. They're so inspiring—the colors they use, the way they wear their clothes or their jewelry, even the amounts of jewelry they wear. It's totally different from anything here in the States." Once again, Tabra now travels with her son, Tangi, who shares his mother's marvel of foreign lands and sometimes accompanies her. He is twenty-nine and a strikingly handsome and statuesque man with long, dark hair. Tangi is also employed at the Tabra Company offices.

Tabra has had a wild life; hard work, diligence, and vision has made her business wildly successful. During our day together Tabra discussed her life as an entrepreneur, artist, mother, and world traveler, and what it means to be a single woman turning fifty.

*I*MAKE BEAUTIFUL JEWELRY BECAUSE IT INTERESTS ME. I'm not making it so women will feel good; I'm making it because it pleases me. I want my business to grow so that I can hire more refugees. Many of them who come to this country are being taken advantage of; I think it's extremely important for America's soul to take in refugees and to treat them well.

The direction this country has gone in during the past twelve years under Reagan and Bush is horrifying. There's so much in the world that is terrible, especially the wars. I can't stop wars but I can make this company a better place for the people who work here. We must learn to not just tolerate other cultures but to appreciate and learn from them.

Our employees are encouraged to use their special interests in the company. For example, our receptionist, Priscilla, is a vegetarian and is sensitive to animals' rights. So she makes sure that we don't use any products that are tested on an animal. White Out was being tested on animals, so we no longer use that product. Our Personnel Manager, Joyce, is especially interested in people with disabilities, so she's going to seminars to learn about starting a program here for the disabled. I'm very interested in gay rights, so we've had four people who are gay or lesbian come and speak to all the workers and management. We had a Latino for the Latin Americans; we had a Laotian, a Vietnamese, and an American speak to individual groups. At one point I told the workers that we *would* be hiring gays. Earlier, a gay man had come to the workroom, and there had been a lot of snickering, so I felt it was time to address that issue. We've also had people speak to us about AIDS because we would like to hire someone who has AIDS or is HIV-positive. The president of our company has four young children, within a year apart, so he's getting on the board of an organization that helps single mothers find jobs and get off welfare. Those are the kinds of things I want to encourage here.

I think I see life from a world view rather than only from an American view. By working with so many different people from so many countries and through traveling so much, I don't feel so American. In many ways the country doesn't matter—we're all people, that's an important message. Wars are caused by the fact that we think other people's ways are not as good as ours, and that we don't have anything to learn from them. If we can get along here at my company, I'll be more hopeful about the world.

We're coming out of the recession very, very slowly. We've done better than anyone else I know of in this particular field of art jewelry. We're doing well although we're no longer doubling—just holding our own. I try to come up with new designs all the time; that's important—to keep them fresh. You can't continue to make the same thing and hope people will keep buying it. The only way for me to keep the designs flowing is to take these trips. Without my trips to exotic countries, the ideas quit. I like to take two or three trips a year, to be out of the country for at least two months. I almost feel like I *have* to get out; if I don't, it all stops.

The wilder the better; I definitely want to get to New Guinea and I want to go farther into Africa—anywhere that is totally alien to what I know. I want to go to the tribal dances in New Guinea; that's what really inspires me and comes out in my jewelry. Unfortunately, the jewelry that sells the best is not necessarily the jewelry that is inspired—the heavy, tribal pieces I make don't sell as well. Americans are more into glitzy. Some of my best-selling jewelry are the shiny, glitzy ones that I don't even like and I wouldn't wear. If I decide that my mission here is to help some refugees get jobs and to see them flourish, then should I turn down opportunities to make things that sell? That would be selfish, and yet I can't grow if I have to keep making little star and moon jewelry with glittery beads on them. The only way I can grow is to keep making the ones that *don't* sell. Then I can be a good artist, and that's important to me too.

I like human hair to be on the pieces, and bone and teeth and snake vertebrae and Hands of Fatima—things to ward off evil and things that are voodoo; that's what interests me. I haven't actually studied those things like voodoo, but I like to float through a country and kind of absorb it. I get an idea in one country and an idea in another country—I see something in Africa and then another thing in Asia and it all churns around in my head and comes out earrings.

My forties have been very difficult; I hope my fifties will be better. I am extremely angry at the fact that most men my age are looking for much younger women—twenty years younger! *Thirty* years younger!—they are not interested in women their own age. In trying to find a man who is good for me, I've joined the dating service Great Expectations. I've also put ads in newspapers as well as answered them. Most men won't admit it but they're threatened by my success. I'm not particularly popular with men. First of all, most of them irritate me. I invariably end up with men who are wrong for me. My friends don't think I should be going out with Latino men because they try to tell me what to do, but they are the ones who turn me on, and if I don't have one who turns me on, why bother? I certainly don't need their money. I'm very happy when I don't have a man, and I'm usually miserable when I do. But that's because I find the wrong kind. I date nice men; I just don't date them twice. I've been in therapy for thirteen years and I understand a lot more now. I'm going to change this pattern—but it's very difficult.

I've always felt kind of plain, so I dress myself like a gypsy and it makes me feel more interesting, but as you get into your forties and fifties, men are not looking for interesting women, they're looking for cutie-pies, and I'm not. I've tried playing down what I do and also telling *exactly* what I do. It doesn't seem to make any difference. It's like real estate, except you're trying to sell yourself. I'm not interested in being a housewife—I don't cook and I certainly wouldn't iron anyone's shirt for him. What I want is an equal partner—they don't have to make lots of money but I'd like them to pay for themselves because I'm tired of paying for both of us. I want to travel to Third World, exotic countries and I'd like someone to go with me, to have fun with me, without telling me what to do. Unfortunately, with men, it seems like just a matter of time before they start telling you what to do. I do so well without one; I don't know why I even want one.

I lived with a Japanese man for five years. I lived with a Trinidadian off and on for five years; I was engaged to him. I lived with a Chicano guy for five years and my Samoan husband for five years. In between I had Africans, more Japanese, and Chinese—those are the kind of men who have appealed to me. At least I've been consistent. I try to date white men but it doesn't work out too well. I'm working on Anglos. My personal relationships with men have just been disasters. My life is successful in just about every other area except this one, and relationship is a huge one—it can ruin the rest of it. My women friends are so good to me. Why should I put up with a man treating me poorly when my closest friends treat me so well? They've given me so much confidence.

I'm learning better to accept my aging; at first it was overwhelming to lose my looks and I became horridly paranoid. Every month, it seemed, I looked a little worse, I'd discover something new that was ugly and then it became every week and then every day and then every minute. I thought, "I'm getting uglier and there's nothing I can do about it." I see older women who I admire because they interest *me,* so why wouldn't a man be interested? So I'm finally learning to accept being fifty. How will I deal with my fifties? I don't know; it's very hard for me just dealing with how I look: trying to fix it up and keep it. I think parents program us when we're very young: anything that isn't perfect on you, they want you to fix. I know my father always told me I would never find a man if I didn't get my teeth fixed and do *some*thing with my hair. Well, I've never been able to get the hair to do what it should and sure enough I don't have a man, so somewhere in my mind, there's that connection between perfection and happiness. I thought "If only I could make myself pretty enough I'd get the right man"; the hair was the main thing. So I'd end up with all these men with beautiful hair. But the price I paid was too high, and now that I'm almost fifty, what I'm discovering is that maybe I don't have to have a man, and that I don't have to be that beautiful because my women friends like me fine just the way I am.

Women in their forties and fifties are not valued in our society, so if you're going to make it at all, you've got to be exceptional—otherwise they treat you as if you hardly exist. Women are valued so much for their young bodies; when you no longer have a youthful body, who are you? You're ignored. Well, I don't want to be ignored, so here in my company, they can't ignore me. I have men working for me, but I have a lot more women.

In my fifties I plan to stay as healthy as I can because I want to be one of those women who is eighty years old and still traveling around the world. It's hard to travel in those exotic countries—even at my age it's difficult. I try to do some form of exercise for an hour each day, but when I travel my routine gets disrupted. When I get back I have to start it up again, because how can I keep going into the jungles and into primitive areas and sleeping on the ground or whatever it is that I have to do if I'm not in good condition? Physically, I'm in better shape than I've ever been. I hope that continues, because in my thirties I was starting to get sloppy and flabby from sitting around making jewelry for all those years and eating poorly and not exercising. Unfortunately, I'm addicted to chocolate and sweets, but other than that I'm very good. I hardly ever get sick and when I travel, I can pretty much eat what I want and drink the water without it affecting me adversely. Healthwise I seem to be fine, although mentally I may be going!

In your fifties, you can start concentrating on things that are really important and give up on those things that are unimportant, like trying to look very sexy and hoping to get a man by looking a certain way. You can start concentrating on things that have always interested you and that you've wanted to accomplish. You waste a lot of time in your thirties trying to look twenty and in your forties trying to look thirty.

When I was twenty, I was very flat-chested. I was so uncomfortable with my body, because you see the pictures of full-breasted women in *Playboy* magazine, and I would hear men talking and laughing about women as if they weren't really women because they didn't have large breasts. I did everything I could think of, all kinds of exercises and bras, nothing worked—I just wasn't built that way. When I was twenty-five I went to live in Costa Rica. Because of an allergy I went to see a doctor. As it turned out, he was a gynecologist who was expanding his practice to include plastic surgery. He saw how flat-chested I was and, even though he'd never done a silicone breast-implant operation before, I decided to be the guinea pig. I had an affair with the doctor and later found out he had affairs with almost all his patients. He definitely took advantage of me. I was very young and he was quite a bit older. He did the operation for free—the only thing I had to do was take "before and after" pictures so they could show other patients the difference. Fortunately the breasts came out fine.

It wasn't like I looked fantastic; it was more like I looked normal to myself, and I looked more like a woman because I associated breasts with women—and who wouldn't in our society with *Playboy*-type magazines and such as our gauge for attractiveness. The anger has built up in me because I realized I had this operation for *men*. They have their fantasies about women, and I put my life on the line to please them. As I got older, my breasts hardened more and more, but I got used to them because I didn't know what real breasts felt like. When you first get to know a man, he goes for the breasts; after that, he forgets about them. I believe that's true. Some men actually prefer small ones. You always have to worry—there are so many different kinds of fantasies that men have; trying to figure out their fantasies and then mold yourself into it is the kind of thing that makes women go mad.

Two years ago, a friend told me, when we were trying on clothes, that my breasts didn't look natural and that I needed to go to a doctor. We went together and I had the silicone breasts taken out and new ones (with a saline solution) put in. They had to scrape my chest to get out all the silicone that had leaked out and hardened over the years. The six-hour operation left me weak from the anesthesia for a long time. It wasn't horribly painful but it was extremely uncomfortable—I couldn't sleep for weeks because it would hurt when I'd move. I stayed at a friend's house and she took care of me.

Then I could see that they didn't look right to me after that second operation, they didn't look pretty like they had the first time. I told the doctor they didn't look right and he kept saying, "Wait a few months, be patient." I waited some months and went back to him again. When I complained, he said, "Tabra, you're going to give me a bad reputation. Give it time." I look at them now and they look okay, but they certainly don't look like what you would expect for $10,000. You want perfect ones. You want them to look like they would if you were twenty. They don't. But I would rather have them than no breasts, which is practically what I had naturally. And I would rather have them than the silicone breasts, which were not healthy. The doctor said he could do the operation again and he would work on making them a little more perfect. But I don't want to go through it again; I keep thinking, "They're good enough. They're as good as any other woman my age, and that should be good enough." I guess being an artist makes me a perfectionist. When I make a pair of earrings, I work on it and it gets better and better. With my body, I can work on it and work on it, but it doesn't get better—it just gets older. I'm not ready to give up therapy because I'm still working on trying to accept the aging process, and therapy helps me.

It just makes me angry that we're told when we are young that we have to look good all the time in order to get a man; once you've got him, you can relax, but you have to find him first. It keeps you nervous all the time, trying to fix yourself up, and then it makes your aging process so difficult because you've been told you aren't acceptable unless you can make yourself look good, and you can no longer make yourself look that good. Women my age are desperately trying to look like pictures in the magazines that *those* women themselves don't even look like.

I see women my age getting better and better and more intelligent and with a stronger set of morals. I'm a better person than I've ever been, I'm able to make a contribution, and yet I get less and less appreciation from the majority of men. And the society as a whole. Isn't is supposed to be about learning and growing? But the more you learn and grow, the more successful you become, the less valuable you are if you're a woman. You can feel this even when you're thirty. I remember someone asking me if I was going on for a doctorate. I said, "No, it's hard enough to find a man when you have a master's." I can recall thinking, "I'm sure not going to work on a doctorate because I *already* intimidate men." What a thing, because it keeps women from wanting to succeed.

DR. LORRAINE HALE

I no longer think in terms of how much time I might have to accomplish what I need to do. Now I think, I'll do as much as I can and just keep pushing. I'm laying plans. The fifties are a wonderful time during which to make those plans. For me it has been a transitional period.

profile

"I've been interviewed by people, but no one ever wanted to put me in a book!" Dr. Lorraine Hale told me. "Are you sure you don't have me confused with Mother?" "Mother" is Clara Hale, founder of Hale House, located in Central Harlem in New York City. Now eighty-seven years old, Mother Hale raised more than forty children as a foster parent between the years of 1941 and 1968. In 1969 she took in her first newborn drug-addicted baby. Since that time Hale House has provided a home for more than eight hundred children.

Lorraine Hale has a doctorate in child development from Western University and has been running Hale House for the past twenty-two years. She tells me that only fourteen of the nearly one thousand children resident at Hale House have been voluntarily placed by their parents in preadoptive homes; the rest have been returned to their families, primarily maternal grandmothers. The problems of these innocent children are increasing. Lorraine told me that over 50,000 children have been born to chemically addicted women, and there are presently approximately 28,000 female addicts of childbearing age in New York City alone.

According to Lorraine, the goals of Hale House include: providing care for these children while their parents undergo rehabilitation; reuniting them with their families; and doing research to understand the long-term effects of addictive drugs on infant growth and development.

We sat in Lorraine's third-story office in Harlem, where I assured her I had not confused her with Mother, and encouraged her to tell me the story of her life.

"I haven't thought about my childhood in so long," reminisced Lorraine. "It was safe. I was safe. And I was happy." She remembers going to school and not liking it very much, but going anyway. Her mother enrolled her in the first grade when she was only four years old. "I don't know what she told people, but I was tall for my age and she said I needed all the education I could get." At some point Lorraine skipped a couple of grades; she's still not sure whether it was because she was bright or because she was tall. Mother Hale kept her daughter a youngster. She made it clear that Lorraine was not a miniature adult—she was a kid. Lorraine says her mother was friendly to her but was not her friend. However, they eventually became best friends, "so it didn't quite work out the way she had planned."

Mother and daughter always spent a great deal of time together and all through Lorraine's growing up years shared many activities. Because they were very poor, they did a lot of walking. Whether they lived in what is now known as Spanish Town, on the East Side in the nineties, or in Harlem, they always walked arm-in-arm to buy food at the market that still stands at 116th Street. "We rarely bought meat," Lorraine recalled. "We ate only vegetables and fruit, potatoes and rice—perhaps chicken on Sundays." A good diet, exercise, and an abundance of love kept Lorraine and her brother, Nathan, healthy. "We were too poor to get sick, Mother would remind us from time to time. 'Don't you *dare* get sick!' I think we had a very nice life, a very good life," said Lorraine.

The good life continues at Hale House, a five-story impeccably neat brownstone on West 122nd Street. On the day of my visit during a sultry September I was directed to the "awards" room (which doubles as a waiting room), where countless plaques, trophies, photographs, and documents line the walls, floor to ceiling. The awards commemorate and pay tribute to both Mother Hale and Lorraine for their service to the community. Lorraine led me upstairs, where twelve to fifteen children live at a time, staying from six to eighteen months. All the furniture in the children's section is in miniature, suitable for children's use: the beds, tables, toilets, and sinks. Even the Oreo cookies are a third the size of regular cookies. Mother Hale's luxurious room is always open to the children and they visit her there often, although, at eighty-nine, Mother Hale now needs around-the-clock care herself. She no longer bounds up and down the five stories, but she still holds, caresses, and soothes crying babies. I spent the afternoon with Lorraine, the beatific Mother Hale, and Jesse, Lorraine's husband. After our lunch of grilled cheese sandwiches, I watched as Lorraine patiently and lovingly cared for her mother and responded to her needs. The tables had turned. The child had become the mother, but they were still friends.

I WAS BORN IN PHILADELPHIA. Because I was a sickly child, I stayed in the hospital for three months after my birth. I was born at home, but the doctor said I was turning blue and took me to the hospital. Meanwhile, my parents moved to New York. My father was extremely ambitious; he had gone to college and later opened his own business. Because he was having stomach problems, he went to stay with his mother back in Philadelphia; he died of stomach cancer ten days later. I was only six years old when he died, so I didn't know him very well, but he spent a lot of time trying to teach me how to read. My brother, who was one and a half years older than me, would read to me. At one point my parents told him to stop reading to me or else I would never learn to read myself. I cried and cried and thought, "I'll show her," and I learned to read. I've gone through life with that sense of "I'll show them."

I was a frightened child. You wouldn't believe that today, but I was. I learned about race relations early; I was scared to death of people who weren't black because I thought somebody was gonna lynch me. I lived in Harlem and, of course, no one was lynched there, so I don't know where that fear came from. But it was real. My mother always told me, "When you come home, everything is safe." Home was the place I went when I couldn't go anywhere else. When my heart was heavy, I went home, and I was always welcome.

I had a close relationship with my mother; we spent time together and did things together, despite the fact that Mother always took care of other people's children. We were very, very poor, so we walked everywhere. New York was a safe place in the 1930s and '40s. And I was happy.

I became "Big Sis" to many of the children my mother cared for, and I enjoyed the role, although I was never asked to babysit. Whatever I did with the children I did because I wanted to. I don't think I was ever jealous of the children. I felt good about having them around. In fact, I would have preferred if they had stayed forever, but they didn't, and it seemed to me that I was always saying goodbye. It really broke my heart every time. Since Mother has been sick, she's had so many visitors—the doorbell never stops ringing. All those children, who are now adults, sit and talk with her. Even though her memory is fading, she still remembers every one of them.

One day I saw a young woman sitting in a doorway with a baby in her arms. Her head was nodding in the way that heroin addicts do, as if they're sleeping. She was sitting on the same street my mother lived on, and I gave her my mother's address and told her to go there and let Mother take care of her child. That was the beginning of Hale House.

I was a single woman until I was thirty-nine. I'd known Jesse, my husband, for a number of years—we sang in the church choir together, but we hadn't seen each other for a while. One day I ran into him at church and we started seeing each other. I knew he was a nice person and could offer me the kind of grounding I needed because I was always ten feet in the air, reaching for the stars, wanting to find out as much as I could. Jesse is a patient person and I'm not. His instincts are so kind. I'm glad I know him.

What amazes me about aging is that I've finally discovered there are people younger than me. My secretary, Renée, is forty; I'm at least ten years older than she is. I think, "Wow, what happened? Where did the time go?" That discovery was a surprise: to realize that I'm older, but don't feel like it. Also, I realize that I've learned a lot, and I'm willing to share it, but in my own way. I'm around many young people, and I tell them, "I can't tell you the answer, you tell *me* the answer, and then let's see if we agree." That's my style. I think my footsteps are big. You can walk in them, but you have to find your own way. You have to realize your own reality and your own truth. There are too many clones in this world, too many people who have forgotten how to think. We don't need more of those people; we need more people who want to see how the world works. I've learned not to take it all so seriously. It seems the same mistakes are made year after year, very often by the same people. But the world doesn't stop because a mistake is made. The world continues.

I've grown to like me. I think I've made a contribution to the world—it's small, but it's a contribution—I'm pleased with that. Being alive, for me, means helping other people, and I try hard to help. Last week I had a call from a young woman who used to be my secretary—she had just received a promotion. She told me, "I want to thank you; it was because of you and the demands you made on me that I have been able to do well in my life." In my way I did make demands. I kept saying, "You can do it." That's what my mother did with me. People who have worked with me have done well.

Life's been very good. It has its problems: we have hurricanes, we have storms, and then the sun comes out and it's sunny again. That's the way life is. If we're looking for a smooth ride, it doesn't happen. There will be highs, lows, and plateaus, but we live to have an opportunity to climb every mountain in our path. We have an opportunity to embrace the world, to embrace other people, to love other people.

I was always trying to solve the problems of the world, particularly when I was young. When I lived in Mexico, I was going to teach every Mexican to speak English. It never occurred to me that I should learn to speak Spanish! I went to Israel with some girlfriends when I was seventeen and stayed on a kibbutz. I wanted to help them develop a country. Two years ago I was invited back to Israel as a guest of the country. I enjoyed it immensely and learned a lot. I came back home and incorporated in my work some of the things I learned.

We recently developed a program in Harlem called the Tribunal, in which boys and girls who have gotten into scrapes in school—not criminal justice types, but borderline—are brought before a panel or jury of their peers. It's not a question of whether they are guilty or innocent. When you come before the panel, you have done something and you just try to explain why. Children don't have trouble in a vacuum—it's a family problem—so we have to work with the entire family. I also learned from Israeli social workers not to bring families into our office, but to go to the family's home where they are more comfortable and relaxed. The Tribunal has been quite successful. We ask men in the community who work with their hands (plumbers, carpenters, electricians), entrepreneurs who have their own businesses, to contribute to our apprenticeship programs. So the youngsters between the ages of thirteen and fifteen, who get into trouble and are given a sentence of maybe three months of community service, will be in the apprentice program where they can learn a skill and stay busy. The younger ones have to wash graffiti off churches and other public buildings. None of these children are children of addicts, that we know of. They come from fairly stable families. A mother and father are both usually in the home, and are aware enough to see that there's a problem they need help with.

Then I was in Africa to help liberate Africans! I went to the University of Ghana and studied African history. I really enjoyed it, and discovered while I was there that I am American—an unhyphenated American. It was an important trip. I came back with an entirely different perspective—I fully understood that I could do anything I wanted because I was American. Whatever America has, I am entitled to as much as I can ingest. I no longer feel an imaginary ceiling blocking me over my head.

My vision of old age is frightening. Frightening. I hadn't thought about it until Mother became ill. I am now grateful to that doctor who helps people die. I couldn't understand this before, but now I can. To be old is, in many instances, for people to lose all their sense of who they are, to lose their sense of privacy and self-respect. When you are unable to care for yourself physically, somebody else has to do it. Who are you then? Who are you when somebody else has to make decisions you can no longer make for yourself? What is the quality of your life? Some may say, "They're still alive." But are they? We give people medication and we don't know whether it works or not. We just give it to them. Senior citizens should not be seen as experimental animals.

What I've learned has made me somewhat bitter about what is happening to seniors. I look at Mother and thank God I'm there to preserve, to the extent I can, her dignity and her sense of who she is. Aging in a highly technological society has become totally dehumanized. Wasn't it nicer before, when people were permitted to live in dignity and to die in dignity without having to feel that life must be prolonged forever?

Our seniors should not have to beg for money; they helped to build this country. Whether they stayed home and just took care of children, or whether they went out to work everyday, it is because of their efforts that America exists. Our resources should be offered to them. And I don't say that just because I'm getting old; I sincerely believe it.

The fifties have been remarkably good to me. That's when I grew up; I became an adult. I became responsible for who I am, for what I do, for what I say. I plan to continue to do that. I smell roses now. I see trees. I know what the sun means. I take time to see everything that goes on in the natural world around me. I don't read about it in a book anymore; I experience it. I'm fortunate to live in a house and on land that I own. I look forward to the next few years. If ever there was a time for me to teach, this is it. The problem is that colleges don't want anyone in their fifties and sixties. In fact they want them out, but this is the time when I *really* have something to say.

I've never had my own children. My mother enjoyed raising all those children, that's what she wanted to be doing, but I would never want to do that. She had no time for herself. I wanted time for me. I liked going to school and I wanted to have time for that. I finally realized what the great drama was for me about not having children: it had to do with saying "goodbye." I would have to say goodbye to my children and let them go out and live their lives. Also, there was the issue of racism. I wasn't sure I wanted to raise children in a country where you are judged by the color of your skin. I wanted my children to be free to love, to be loved, to experience whatever they wanted to experience.

And then, of course, there was the experience I had when I was fourteen. That *really* did it. There was a black man in Harlem who killed his two sons, because he said he could not raise boys in America. I was young enough to be very impressionable. I knew enough about racial problems to say, "Yeah, that's real. I don't want to have children." It wasn't until I came back from Africa that I realized I could determine how far I wanted to go in my life. *Now* I feel I have that freedom in America.

As I take care of my mother, I have been very watchful of her, yet I have not been able to say, "I wish I had a child to do that for me" because perhaps I wouldn't. You don't have children to take care of you; you have children so they can be free like butterflies to experience the world. I haven't thought that the day would come when I would say, "I wish I had someone to get me a glass of water." I just hope I'll be able to get it myself until my time comes. I don't dwell on death, although I'm thinking about it more now because of Mother's illness. But I'm more concerned with what I can do tomorrow.

Last month I was quite sick for a few weeks. I was pleased to realize that you don't just get sick—there are warning signs if you heed them—there is a tiredness, a depression, and I wasn't cognizant of it before. Suddenly, I was very tired and attributed everything to getting old. I began singing that sad song, "You're not going to be able to do anything anymore." Then I realized that was not it. Something was happening to my body and it was giving me messages. I no longer think in terms of how much time I might have to accomplish what I need to do. Now I think, "I'll do as much as I can and just keep pushing." I'm laying plans. Thank God for this period of time. The fifties are a wonderful time during which to make those plans. For me it has been a transitional period.

Getting older is inevitable. It's important to grow with it, make peace with it, continue to do your life's work and be proud you have lived this long and learned so much. I think I'm more spiritual now than I've ever been. I believe we're all here for a purpose and it's our responsibility to fulfill that purpose. If you didn't have time to discover it when you were younger, now is the time to do that and move toward it. As younger women we always had the excuses, "I'm in school," or "I'm married," or "I have children." It's easy to get morose, to stay in your pity party and say, "I'm getting older and I can't do anything about it." I think you *can,* and I think you can do it by yourself. What gives us the desire to go on living? It's the hope that we can make tomorrow brighter for someone else. I'm grateful that I'm healthy, glad that I can get up in the morning and make my own decisions. I'm pleased that I can drive a car and get myself to work. Hope springs eternal. There's so much we can do. We just have to get out and start doing it.

Mother says I was born with a veil over my eyes—it's just a membrane that covers the fetus. There is a superstition that those born with this "veil" are seers. For many years when I was a child, people would ask me different questions about the future. I would always have an answer. I think everyone has their own way of knowing; I may exercise mine more than other people. There are things you just know. And, as we get older, much of what we know is from experience. Buoyed with that information, it's still my world and I'm out there trying to capture stars.

DR. JEAN
SHINODA BOLEN

I think there is an increased authenticity and autonomy in turning fifty. I've been struck by how women in the Women's Movement define themselves against whatever the cultural expectation is at every decade. We are now postmenopausal and have a different view of what this period might be. We're discovering it.

profile

I have always thought of a myth as something that never was but is always happening.
JEAN HOUSTON, *The Possible Human*

JEAN SHINODA BOLEN BELIEVES THAT WE ARE "spiritual beings on a human path," that the choices we make in life matter. She also believes in the existence of personal myths—the power to create and define one's own story as one progresses through life. She also believes that these personal myths are informed by and metaphors for the collective unconscious "stash" of multicultural narratives. If we can be aware of our own story as it unfolds, we have a better chance of understanding and making friends with our life.

Mythology, metaphor, menopause, motherhood, archetypes, persona, pilgrimage, psychology of women, consciousness, dreams, synchronicity, symbols, patterns, human potential, gods and goddesses—these were some of the subjects of my dialogue with Jean Bolen. Even our meeting itself, in her San Francisco office, was steeped in myth: it was the week of Easter, which commemorates the Resurrection of Christ, is synchronized with the Jewish Pesach, and blends since the earliest days of Christianity with pagan European rites for rebirth and the renewed season. We were engaged in a ritual of reenacting the myth of the Wise Woman, crone or female sage as teacher to the willing student. It was easy to see its alchemical process at work: recognizing and honoring that older women have significant and valuable knowledge to share with younger women.

Jean Shinoda Bolen is the author of *The Tao of Psychology; Goddesses in Everywoman; Gods in Everyman;* and *Ring of Power: The Abandoned Child, The Authoritarian Father, and the Disempowered Feminine.* She is also a psychiatrist and Jungian analyst in private practice in San Francisco, and teaches at the University of California Medical Center and the San Francisco Jung Institute. In addition, she is a lecturer and workshop leader, and is reputed to be a gifted storyteller.

In *Goddesses in Everywoman,* Jean Bolen divided seven major Greek goddesses into three primary categories: the virgin goddesses, the vulnerable goddesses, and the alchemical (or transformative) goddess. The virgin goddesses, Artemis, Athena, and Hestia, represent the independent, self-sufficient quality in women who actively seek their own goals. The vulnerable goddesses, Hera, Demeter, and Persephone, represent the traditional roles of wife, mother, and daughter. The alchemical goddess, Aphrodite, the Goddess of Love and Beauty, is in a category all her own. It is Jean's premise—in what she calls "a new psychology of women"—that goddesses representing all three categories need expression somewhere in a contemporary woman's life in order for her to love deeply, work meaningfully, and be sensual and creative.

Jean is reserved by nature, and at first I found it difficult to get a personal sense of the woman behind the professional persona. It was only when she would suddenly let out an uncharacteristically girlish giggle in response to something one of us had said that I caught a glimpse into another side of the Jungian analyst. For several hours I listened and observed as this diminutive woman, who has been a mother, wife, medical doctor, Jungian analyst, teacher, lecturer, writer, and traveler, dipped into her symbolic cauldrons of experience, compassion, and vision. It would seem that she has personally experienced each of the seven Greek goddess archetypes about which she has written: Persephone, as daughter and voyager to the Underworld (as a Jungian analyst probing the unconscious realm); Hera, as wife; Demeter, as mother; Athena, as a woman who has succeeded in the traditionally male occupation of psychiatry; Aphrodite, as a creative woman, lover, and carrier of visions; Artemis, as a woman who is independent, an ardent feminist, and a lover of travel to distant and foreign places; and Hestia, as a woman who is "one-unto-herself" and seeks the tranquility that solitude provides. According to Jean, "Which goddess or goddesses (several may be present at the same time) become activated in any particular woman at any particular time depends on the combined effect of a variety of interacting elements—the woman's predisposition, family and culture, hormones, other people, unchosen circumstances, chosen activities, and stages of life."

Mid-life is a time of transition on many levels. Although there may be assorted women who suffer from the "empty-nest" syndrome, anthropologist Margaret Mead vouched for numerous other women pulsating with "postmenopausal zest." In *Goddesses in Everywoman,* Jean notes that "this upsurge can happen when a newly energized goddess can now have her long-awaited turn." As a single woman myself, I identified with Jean when she demonstrated how as a woman currently living without a man, she feels the archetypal presence of solitary Hestia, the Wise Woman who "represents the Self, an intuitively known spiritual center of a woman's personality that gives meaning to her life."

According to Martha Farnsworth Riche, director of policy studies at the nonprofit Population Reference Bureau in Washington, D.C., "Generally, *the happiest people are single women* [italics mine], followed by married men, then married women. The least happy are single men." Could the idea of Hestia as a companion in solitude help to bring other single women the sense of comfort and pleasure in their own company that Jean and (perhaps even without their knowing) the women in this study have experienced?

In an interview the painter Mayumi Oda described to me how her creative process is a means to personal transformation. "I think the creative process is about creating who *I* am. In other words, I create myself through my creation, through my creative activity." A few years earlier, she'd had "a tremendous urge" to produce a book called *Goddesses*. When she began thinking "Why?" it became clear to her when she realized, "My Goddess! This is what I want to be, so I have created it."

Jean understands the workings of mythic patterns active in all our lives—even among those of us who do not recognize them or may even discount them—and supported Mayumi's observation when she said, "It is possible to 'invoke' a goddess, by consciously making an effort to see, feel, or sense her presence—to bring her into focus through your imagination—and then ask for her particular strength." Had Jean successfully "invoked" goddesses in her own life? And, if so, how? These questions provided a colorful and intriguing context for a Good Friday afternoon well spent together.

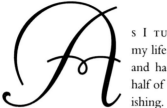As I turned forty-nine, major shifts occurred in my life. I brought an end to a long marriage, moved, and had my then adolescent children live with me half of the time. I found solitude unexpectedly nourishing. I lost my former clear sense of myself and my future, and gained access to feelings and aspects of myself that I'd lost. My spiritual life then took on a whole new dimension—that of a pilgrimage. Pilgrimage was not something I thought of or intended, rather it was a pure gift, an invitation extended to me.

I was invited to come to the Netherlands to be part of a private audience with the Dalai Lama, and then to go to Chartres Cathedral in France, and from there to sacred places in England and Scotland. This was my first pilgrimage. Over the next two years, I would go to Greece, India, and Ireland, and I would meet Mother Teresa, Dadi Jahnke, Archbishop Runcie, and many other people on various spiritual paths. The life-changing experience of pilgrimage was not about who I met or where I went. It was what happened to me that was profound.

First at Chartres Cathedral, and then at other sacred places around the globe, I found myself responding in my body to the energy that was there. Up to then, knowledge and perceptions came to me through my mind or heart, through feelings, thoughts, or intuitions. Now my body was the instrument through which I felt a connection to the Earth, and in some ineffable way, I knew that places of pilgrimage were changing me, as if the molecules of my soul were being affected. These experiences embodied my psyche—linking soul-body-psyche altogether—in some wonderful way that is a mystery that I keep discovering as I go along.

I would turn fifty on returning from my first pilgrimage, not knowing at the time, of course, that I had had my last menstrual period in Glastonbury, England. Menopause was not a difficult transition for me. I now wonder if the communication between my body and sacred places, between my earth and the Earth at those sites, had something to do with the ease with which I entered menopause.

I marvel at the meaningful coincidence, the synchronistic timing that I was invited to go on pilgrimage. Had I not been separated, I doubt very much that I would have spent so much time away from my family; but when the invitation came, my children lived with me only half of the time. It also was shortly after I had read *The Mists of Avalon*. Glastonbury was where Morgaine called the barge to cross the mists to Avalon, and I was at that time being drawn increasingly into the spiritual realm of the goddess. I had written *Goddesses in Every Woman* from a psychological perspective, and found that by evoking the archetypal goddesses, that it opened the door to the spiritual dimension of the goddess.

For me, synchronicity is sometimes obvious; other times, I wonder if something could be synchronistic, and I think about it as I would a dream. There are big synchronicities and big dreams that are hard to discount, and others that we get something from if we pay attention. I know that life is just more fascinating when we pay attention to them and wonder what they are telling us.

I like the saying, "Synchronicity is God acting anonymously." When they happen, there is a real sense of connectedness, that we are part of a greater universe, and that there is meaning in life.

I am in a major creative time in my professional life, which has three parts—my practice, writing, lectures and workshops—each of which adds significantly to the others, all of which I love to do. It's a wonderful combination, and it works well as long as I keep it balanced and make time for my personal life. My practice is limited to only three days a week. Writing is something I do for stretches at a time, and I travel to lectures, conferences, and workshops as scheduled, anticipating a new experience each time.

I didn't start out to be a Jungian analyst, or a psychiatrist for that matter. Idealism and perseverance kept me in medicine in spite of my liberal leanings. Finding my way to psychiatry and Jungian analysis, however, took synchronicity and grace.

I took my residency in psychiatry at the University of California Medical Center at Langley-Porter, not because I knew I wanted to be a psychiatrist, but because at the time it enabled me to return to San Francisco. I began in the acute treatment service with hospitalized psychotic or suicidally depressed patients, and found that I really could care about these people. They didn't scare me and I didn't scare them. We could establish rapport and enter into a therapeutic relationship easily. They got better, and I had found work that I loved and had a gift for.

Jungian analysts were on the clinical faculty at UC at that time. There were a few others at only one other residency in the country. Even though there were not many of them, I was randomly assigned two Jungian analysts in my first two years of residency, and would work with another in my third year. As people, the Jungians were more interesting to me. They seemed less uptight than other supervisors, they were interested in dreams, and considered spirituality and creativity appropriate concerns. Thus I gravitated to the Jungian Institute to learn more. When I was accepted, I found I was the only candidate that year, a class of one.

Being a therapist means that anything and everything I've ever experienced may help someone, sometime. A most painful event may be redeemed, if I tap into it in order to connect with someone else. I've arrived at the conclusion that nothing that I have lived goes to waste. To appreciate that this is so, one must have lived long enough.

Writing grew out of my Jungian perspective and the liberal arts person I was all along. I was drawn to write so that I could have some introverted time alone to think, at a time when small children, husband, home, dog, and practice meant I was always relating or caretaking. In order to write, I began getting up early, before the rest of the household was awake.

When I write even now, I get up between five and six in the morning, write for four or five hours, and then go to the office, if it's a working day. Other days I may write for a longer period when I'm on a creative roll. I'm an early bird anyway, so getting up early is no problem, especially when I'm in the midst of a writing project. Right now, I'm not. But, I've got three cauldrons bubbling on my back burners, simmering books that I will someday write. I add ingredients—thoughts, ideas, stories, references, images, tossing them into what is an intuitive process. Usually, a title comes to the surface first, and then the form takes shape, and, as I write, I draw upon what comes.

Speaking was actually my first medium of expression. I was a high school debater and a competitor in extemporaneous speaking, so lectures came easily, leading to workshops, which were initially just longer lectures. Now I know that creating a safe place is the most important element in a workshop; same as in my office. *Temenos,* the Greek word for sanctuary, is what allows truth about who we are, what we feel, and what we have experienced to emerge into consciousness and into spontaneous expression.

There is something about being in a woman's circle that I have learned from; not just from leading women's wisdom workshops, but through participating as a member of two ongoing circles, each of which has met regularly now for over three years. A circle of women is a place where you listen to another woman's truth, and it mirrors back who you are; it's a place where women find their own voice and courage; where true emotion expressed by one, facilitates access for others; a safe place for repressed and undeveloped selves to emerge.

I think that what happens in a circle has always happened in friendships between women. What often hasn't been acknowledged by women is the depth and importance of their friendships with one another. When you're going through a difficult time in your life, who do you confide in? Do you speak to your husband or to your best friend? Who sees you as you really are, and yet knows what you really feel? Men and women do have a tougher time seeing each other. We project an awful lot onto each other, and then can't see the other clearly. Plus, women are acculturated to be a reflection of who a significant man wants her to be, and to also reflect back to him what he wants to see about himself. False mirroring and codependency results.

Part of the difficulty with the middle years for men and women is that there is so much work to do: careers, children, house payments. Couples are too exhausted or too busy to be intimates. Then comes the crisis in the relationship, the situation that is both a danger and an opportunity, the one that leads to a deeper dialogue and a deeper commitment to the marriage or ends the marriage—when the choice to stay or to leave is truly possible.

Increasingly, as we get older, we know people who have died, are dying, or are dealing with a condition that can or will kill them. We are affected, especially when they are people close to us, and close to our age. I become acutely aware of how short life is, and how precious it is, and it seems to me that we are on a soul journey. It matters what we do with this finite life. In this regard I think of us as spiritual beings on a human path, rather than human beings on a spiritual path, and muse about the thought that if this is so, what are we here for? There must be much that a soul can experience only by being human. For now, I hope that I can answer affirmatively, "Did I do what I came for?" Did I learn what I came to learn?"

I am fifty-five now, a fact that is out of synch with how young I feel. This is not what I thought fifty-five would be like—thank goodness!

As we enter our postmenopausal years, those of us who are sound physically and emotionally, and exercise our freedom to choose how we spend our time and with whom, we become increasingly, even outrageously independent women. It's a time to remember abilities and visions and loves that were put on the shelf because of family responsibilities and work. Whether it's because the nest is empty, or you are a single woman again, there are possibilities for growth and change. I know women who are painting, traveling, taking up belly dancing, becoming physically fit, returning to school, running races, having lovers, drumming, starting businesses, or quitting them. It's a very interesting phase, and they are much more interesting women than they used to be, as well.

There is an increased authenticity and autonomy that comes with turning fifty. I've been struck by how women in the Women's Movement define themselves against whatever the cultural expectation is at every decade. We are now postmenopausal and have a different view of what this period might be. We're discovering it.

There is a relationship between who we are becoming on turning fifty, and the three aspects of the Goddess, mythologically. She was maiden, mother, and crone. As archetypes in us, all three feminine aspects are eternally present, though, at any given time, we are biologically only one of them.

I and many other professional women with families lose touch with our own playful, vulnerable, or adventuresome qualities in our thirties and forties. While we were taking care of our actual children, or looking after, or codepending someone else's inner child, our own inner child disappeared. "She" often resurfaces around the time our menses are on the way out, and we are once again as we were in adolescence, in the throes of interior change. Often it seems, too, that child and crone join our competent adult selves around fifty. At which time we may feel and be more "one unto ourselves" than at any other time in our lives.

Workshop and Lecture Announcement

For information on Coming into Our Fullness Workshops and Lectures
please send requests to:

Cathleen Rountree
P.O. Box 552
Aptos, CA 95001

or FAX: 408-685-0211